MAKING SENSE OF
ISAIAH

MAKING SENSE OF
ISAIAH

INSIGHTS AND MODERN APPLICATIONS

TERRY BALL AND NATHAN WINN

DESERET
BOOK

SALT LAKE CITY, UTAH

Library of Congress Cataloging-in-Publication Data
Ball, Terry B.
  Making sense of Isaiah : insights and modern applications / Terry B. Ball and Nathan Winn.
      p.   cm.
  Includes bibliographical references and index.
  ISBN 978-1-60641-000-4 (hardbound : alk. paper)
  1. Bible. O.T. Isaiah—Criticism, interpretation, etc.   2. Church of Jesus Christ of Latter-day Saints—Doctrines.   I. Winn, Nathan.   II. Title.
  BS1515.52B35 2009
  224'.107—dc22
                                                                          2009037042

Printed in the United States of America
Publishers Printing, Salt Lake City, UT

10   9   8   7   6   5   4   3   2   1

CONTENTS

INTRODUCTION

When the resurrected Savior visited the descendants of Lehi gathered at the temple in Bountiful, He quoted Isaiah 54 to them and then gave a remarkable endorsement to the prophet's writings: "Behold, I say unto you, that ye ought to search these things. Yea, a commandment I give unto you that ye search these things diligently; for great are the words of Isaiah" (3 Nephi 23:1).

Many have wished that the Savior had picked an easier text to command us to study. We would prefer that He had said, "Master the writings of Omni!" or "Ponder the words of Ruth!" But the Savior explained why Isaiah's writings were deserving of His special endorsement. He declared, "For surely he [Isaiah] spake as touching all things concerning my people which are of the house of Israel; therefore it must needs be that he must speak also to the Gentiles" (3 Nephi 23:2). Thus, He taught that Isaiah spoke not only to the house of Israel but also to everyone who would hear or read his words. The Savior then added His own testimony of Isaiah's words: "And all things that he spake have been and shall be, even according to the words which he spake" (3 Nephi 23:3).

Knowing that we have been specifically commanded to study Isaiah does not make the text any easier. Many of us view the writings of Isaiah as the brussels sprouts of the scriptures. When they appear on our scriptural plate, we look at them and know that we should partake of them, but we may not be excited about the prospect. Perhaps we race through them as fast as we can, just to finish them. Then we sigh in relief and congratulate ourselves for having accomplished the task, thinking, "I know that was good for me, but I don't know why." Sometimes teachers approach the text with similar apprehension. Typically lacking time to thoroughly cover Isaiah's writings, they choose to talk about how to understand them, offering a few pointers and then moving on to more palatable text. It would be difficult to argue that such approaches fulfill the Savior's admonition to search the prophet's words diligently.

This volume takes another approach. It is not a commentary or a textual analysis but rather an invitation to find applications from Isaiah's writings for our daily lives. It is meant to be read alongside the book of Isaiah itself. First, we provide a brief overview of each chapter of Isaiah to help readers know what to look for as they study the text. Then, following the admonition of Nephi to liken the words of Isaiah to ourselves (1 Nephi 19:23; 2 Nephi 6:5), we present an example of a latter-day application or fulfillment for a part of each chapter. We end each discussion with two or three questions readers may wish to ponder to enhance their understanding and invite the Spirit to guide their thoughts. It is our intent to be illustrative rather than exhaustive in this endeavor. We hope our examples will serve as a stimulus to deeper study, inviting readers to ponder other applications and fulfillments in our day, as well as providing teachers with insights they can readily draw upon as they help their students appreciate this remarkable prophet. We believe that those of us willing to invest the effort to diligently search the words of Isaiah will come to love them—that we can come to view Isaiah as a main course, or even dessert, the part of our scriptural sustenance that we look forward to consuming, savoring, and delighting in every morsel.

ISAIAH THE MAN

Knowing something about Isaiah the man can be helpful in a study of his writings. His name means, literally, "Jehovah is salvation," a central theme in his prophecies. He lived in and prophesied to the kingdom of Judah during the last half of the eighth century before Christ. He also prophesied concerning Judah's sister nation, the kingdom of Israel, as well as such other nations as Syria, Assyria, Babylon, Moab, Egypt, Philistia, and Phoenicia. We think that Isaiah was born about 770 B.C. and received his call as a prophet around 740 B.C., in the days of King Uzziah (6). He enjoyed an exceptionally long tenure as a prophet. There were occupational hazards associated with being a prophet to an apostate people, and Old Testament prophets often did not live long. Remarkably, Isaiah served during the reigns of four kings of Judah: Uzziah, Jotham, Ahaz, and Hezekiah. He likely died around 692 B.C. This means he served as a prophet for almost fifty years—an extraordinary length of time in that era. Tradition holds that he was martyred by being placed in a hollow log and sawn asunder by Hezekiah's wicked son and successor, Manasseh.

Isaiah was an anomaly in other ways as well. Often when we think of an Old Testament prophet, we picture a simple man living a simple life: Elijah, living in the desert, wearing a garment made of camel hair, and being fed by ravens; or Amos of tiny Tekoa, herding sheep and dressing sycomore figs. Isaiah appears to have been different. He seems to have been an aristocratic man who could obtain audience with kings. One tradition holds that Isaiah was actually King Hezekiah's father-in-law. His writings show him to be a highly educated and gifted thinker. Most of his prophecies are couched in beautiful Hebrew poetry. He was a truly sophisticated and remarkable man.

ORGANIZATION OF THE BOOK OF ISAIAH

Scholars often divide the book of Isaiah into three sections. Chapters 1 through 35 are prophecies primarily dealing with judgment and warnings to the people. Chapters 36 through 39 constitute a historical section, chronicling the Assyrian siege of Judah and some other events of the reign of King Hezekiah. Finally, chapters 40 through 66 focus primarily on the greatness of God and the redemption and restoration He offers His people.

Some scholars divide Isaiah's prophecies into sections they see as having different authors. Applying textual criticism, they feel that what they see as different themes and language in the text, as well as the accuracy of the description of events that did not occur until the sixth century before Christ and after, indicate multiple authors. The first, such scholars say, was an Isaiah who lived in the eighth century before Christ and wrote the prophecies of judgment and doom. According to them, the other one or two Isaiahs likely lived during or after the sixth century before Christ and wrote the prophecies of redemption and restoration. These scholars particularly like to ascribe the prophecies dealing with the rise of Babylon as a military power, its conquest and deportation of Judah, and its defeat at the hands of Cyrus, to someone who lived much later than the author of the first chapters of the text. Their conclusions are dictated by a common tenet of textual criticism, which holds that there is no such thing as the supernatural—thus prophets cannot truly foretell the future. Accordingly, if a prophecy is exceptionally accurate, textual critics often conclude it must have been written after the prophesied event occurred and then appended to the text.

Latter-day Saints have reason to question such conclusions in regard to Isaiah, for many of the chapters of Isaiah that these scholars ascribe to an author who lived after the Babylonian captivity (ca. 587–537 B.C.) are quoted in the Book of Mormon. For example, all or part of Isaiah 13–14 and 48–53, chapters often thought to have been written by a later author, are quoted in 1 Nephi 20–21, 2 Nephi 7–8, 13–24, and Mosiah 14. The Book of Mormon prophets and authors knew of these texts from the brass plates, which Lehi and his family had carried with them when they fled Jerusalem before the great Babylonian deportation and captivity. Thus, we see that prophets can foretell future events.

KEYS FOR UNDERSTANDING ISAIAH

The Book of Mormon prophet Nephi loved the writings of Isaiah and quoted from him extensively. For example, he quoted all of Isaiah 2–14 in 2 Nephi 12–24. Students of the Book of Mormon often consider these chapters to be the most difficult in all the Book of Mormon. Many attempting to read the Book of Mormon from cover to cover are stymied in the attempt by the difficulty of the "Isaiah section." Yet, if we persevere and read through to 2 Nephi 25, we find some wonderful suggestions, or keys, for understanding Isaiah's words. Three of the keys for

understanding Isaiah that Nephi mentions are especially helpful. Considering the keys in the reverse order in which Nephi
presents them, we read in 2 Nephi 25:8: "Wherefore, they [the
words of Isaiah] are of worth unto the children of men, and he
that supposeth that they are not, unto them will I speak particularly, and confine the words unto mine own people; for I know
that they [the words of Isaiah] shall be of great worth unto them
in the last days; for in that day shall they understand them."

Thus, one key to understanding Isaiah, according to Nephi,
is to live in the last days. This is a remarkable observation on
his part. Many of us today would want to excuse ourselves from
studying Isaiah by rationalizing that Isaiah lived long ago and
wrote to a different people in a different culture, so we should
not be expected in our day to understand the prophecies well.
Nephi would beg to differ! He declares that our dispensation
should understand the prophet better than any other. Truth
supports Nephi's conclusion. We should indeed better understand Isaiah's writings in our dispensation, for in our day we
have the benefit of historical hindsight and prophetic foresight
to interpret his prophecies, as well as the privilege of viewing his
teachings through the lens and in the light of the fulness of the
restored gospel. Moreover, we live in the time when the writings
of Isaiah find their most complete fulfillment and application.
Truly, we have the means to understand the writings of Isaiah
better than any other dispensation. To take advantage of these
latter-day benefits in our study of Isaiah, it is helpful to discipline ourselves to make a habit of pondering and looking for the
application and fulfillment of Isaiah's writings in our day. Such
was Nephi's admonition when he prefaced some of Isaiah's writings with the instructions, "Hear ye the words of the prophet,

which were written unto all of the house of Israel, and liken them unto yourselves" (1 Nephi 19:24).

Another key to understanding Isaiah is also introduced by Nephi: "My soul delighteth in the words of Isaiah, for I came out from Jerusalem, and mine eyes hath beheld the things of the Jews, and I know that the Jews do understand the things of the prophets, and there is none other people that understand the things which were spoken unto Jews like unto them, save it be that they are taught after the manner of the things of the Jews" (2 Nephi 25:5).

Here Nephi tells us we must know something about "the manner of the things of the Jews" if we are to better comprehend Isaiah. We have found that the "things of the Jews" include their history, culture, literature, theology, art, and language as well as the geology and geography of Israel. Nephi seems to suggest that we need to gather every piece of information we can about Isaiah's culture and day, so we can better put the prophecies in a context that makes sense.

Perhaps such an effort is part of what the Savior had in mind when He commanded us to search the words of Isaiah. It may be helpful to compare the search that Christ commanded to what a detective might do when investigating the scene of a crime. A detective might look for fingerprints, take plaster casts, vacuum for fibers, and ask many questions of witnesses and experts. He will do everything he can think of to gather every shred of information that can help him discover the truth. Such a detailed and thorough search is far different from what a police officer does when he quickly frisks a suspect for weapons. Frisking does not yield many details for the investigator. Likewise, those who simply frisk Isaiah will miss much. We should read the text carefully and gather all the evidence we can to improve our understanding. Such a detailed search might include using footnotes, maps, gazetteers, Bible dictionaries, topical guides, word studies, and commentaries. If we sincerely want to understand Isaiah, we must be willing to pay the price to learn about the "manner of the things of the Jews."

Nephi offered a third key to understanding Isaiah when he declared, "Wherefore, hearken, O my people, which are of the house of Israel, and give ear unto my words; for because the words of Isaiah are not plain unto you, nevertheless they are plain unto all those that are filled with the spirit of prophecy" (2 Nephi 25:4). This third key, to read with the Spirit, is certainly the most important. Wonderful things happen when we study the scriptures under the direction of the Spirit. Feelings come into our hearts, and thoughts come into our minds that teach us truth, doctrine, and applications—often beyond what the author may have consciously intended but, nonetheless, what the Lord would have us learn.

Most of us do several things as we study the scriptures to invite the Spirit into our study. We typically seek out a time and a place to study that is conducive to the promptings of the Spirit, and we pray for guidance and understanding as we study. We have found that one of the most important things we can do to invite the Spirit into our scripture study is to discipline ourselves to ponder as we read. We define pondering as the art of asking questions and thinking about possible answers to those questions. As we ponder such questions as "What is the fulfillment and application of this passage in our day?" "What doctrines are being taught?" or "What do I want to teach my children from these verses?" the Spirit begins to direct our thoughts, and we start to get answers. We get sudden bursts of insight, feelings, and thoughts—we start to receive revelation. It is a marvelous experience and a manifestation that God loves us. He wants us to understand and know His will, and He will readily give us inspiration, guidance, and answers through the Holy Spirit, if we sincerely seek them.

To summarize, then, we learn from Nephi's instructions that we can best understand the writings of Isaiah if we (1) live in the last days and look for the fulfillment and application of the prophecies in our day, (2) make the effort to learn the things of the Jews that will help us place the prophecies in a context that makes sense, and (3) seek the inspiration of the Spirit in our study through prayer and pondering.

A NOTE ON CITATIONS

For ease of reading, we have omitted the quotation marks around single words or short phrases from Isaiah when they appear within a verse that is part of a longer passage being referenced. To streamline citations where clarity is not affected, we have referred to passages in Isaiah only by chapter or by chapter and verse: "(10)" thus means "(Isaiah 10)" and "(13:4)" means "(Isaiah 13:4)." References to a series of whole chapters have semicolons separating the numbers: "(14; 18; 56)" thus means "(Isaiah 14; 18; 56)." Hebrew words and their meanings have not been noted individually; further information may be found in Francis Brown, S. R. Driver, and Charles A. Briggs, *The New Brown-Driver-Briggs-Gesenius Hebrew and English Lexicon with an Appendix Containing the Biblical Aramaic.*

Chapter 1

"THOUGH YOUR SINS BE AS SCARLET"

ISAIAH 1

Isaiah 1 is sometimes called the Great Arraignment, for in it the Lord, in an arraignment-like fashion, lays out His charges against the apostates among Israel.

First, Isaiah and the kings who ruled his native Judah during his ministry are introduced, from Uzziah (ca. 790 B.C.) to Hezekiah (ca. 725 B.C.). Then, at the beginning of the chapter and again at the end, Isaiah outlines the spiritual maladies that trouble the people. With vivid imagery he decries their widespread apostasy and apathy (1:2–6), as well as their hypocrisy and insincerity as they casually, and consequently vainly, go through the motions of worship prescribed in the Mosaic law (1:10–15). He further condemns the people and their leaders for being murderous, rebellious, dishonest, greedy, and lacking in compassion (1:21–23).

As Isaiah describes the people's wickedness, he warns of destruction that will befall them. Speaking of things to come as if they had already occurred (compare Mosiah 16:6), Isaiah foretells the desolation and abandonment that await the people (1:7–9, 20) and promises that the Lord will purge the

11

wickedness from them to redeem Zion and restore her to righteousness (1:24–31).

In typical Hebrew style, the highlight of Isaiah 1 is found
in the middle verses, where the prophet prescribes the spiritual
therapy the people should undergo if they wish to be healed and
offers them a beautiful prognosis of hope (1:16–19).

LIKENING ISAIAH'S WORDS UNTO OURSELVES

The remedy Isaiah prescribes for the wickedness plaguing
the people is good medicine for any spiritual malady in any dispensation. He counsels, "Wash you, make you clean; put away
the evil of your doings from before mine eyes; cease to do evil"
(1:16). In other words, "Repent!" But repentance is not enough.
The people must also "learn to do well; seek judgment, relieve
the oppressed, judge the fatherless, plead for the widow" (1:17).
If the transgressors wish to be healed, they must not only stop
doing wrong but also start doing right—exercising charity by
serving, helping, defending, and loving others, especially those
who are oppressed and destitute.

Through Isaiah, the Lord offers great hope to all who yearn
for forgiveness. "Come now, and let us reason together, saith
the Lord: though your sins be as scarlet, they shall be as white
as snow; though they be red like crimson, they shall be as wool"
(1:18). Many who struggle with the deep sorrow and regret that
initiate repentance wonder if they can ever truly be forgiven.
This promise answers the question as it hints at how such forgiveness is made possible. The imagery of sin being as scarlet reminds us of the atoning blood Christ shed for us as He worked
out the great and infinite atonement on our behalf. The imagery
of wool causes us to think of the whiteness, purity, and inno-
cence of a lamb. Perhaps Isaiah used this imagery to remind us

of the sacred paradox that we may be "washed white through the blood of the Lamb" (Alma 13:11).

QUESTIONS TO PONDER

1. Why do you think Isaiah used the head and the heart for metaphors in describing in 1:5 the spiritual maladies of the people?

2. How can a modern covenant people fall under the same condemnation as that described in 1:10–15?

3. How would you summarize God's plan described in 1:25–27?

Chapter 2

"THE MOUNTAIN OF THE LORD'S HOUSE"

ISAIAH 2

Isaiah 2 records two contrasting prophecies. The chapter opens with the prophet's wonderful vision of the last days, a time when a temple, the mountain of the Lord's house, would be established in the tops of the mountains. He sees that all nations are drawn to the temple to worship and be taught (2:2–3). He further describes the great millennial theocracy of peace that will ensue when the Messiah judges the nations and they forsake violence and war (2:4).

Isaiah then contrasts that wonderful vision of a future of peace, hope, and righteousness with the people's current spiritual state and practices. He condemns them for looking for guidance, instruction, and happiness in the teachings and ways of foreign nations (2:6). He laments their infatuation with wealth and weapons (2:7) and decries their pride and idolatry (2:8–9). With vivid language and imagery he describes the panic, fear, and embarrassment that will befall such wicked people in the "day of the Lord" (2:12).

As he shares these two contrasting visions, Isaiah appears to offer the people a choice. They can persist in iniquity and reap destruction in the day of the Lord, or they can dwell with him in peace and righteousness by choosing to "walk in the light of the Lord" (2:5) rather than trusting in man, "whose breath is in his nostrils" (2:22).

LIKENING ISAIAH'S WORDS UNTO OURSELVES

A mountain is a wonderful metaphor for a temple because each has much in common with the other. If we view a temple as a place of instruction and covenant making, then some mountains, such as Sinai and the Mount of Transfiguration, were indeed temples. Ancient prophets frequently went to mountains to get closer to God and to commune with Him, just as many go to temples today for the same purpose. Mountains draw our attention and help orient us, as do temples for the faithful. Mountains are strong and enduring, as are temple covenants and ordinances. It takes effort to reach the top of a mountain, just as it takes work and effort to qualify to enter a temple. Perhaps most significantly, once we arrive on a mountaintop, we can see the big picture. We can trace the paths we have taken to reach our current place on the mountain, and we can see the paths we must follow to reach our desired destination. So it is with temples. There we gain an eternal perspective. We trace the paths we have followed to reach our current place in mortality and learn of the paths we must follow to reach our eternal goal.

We go to temples to receive an endowment. That endowment can be described as a two-fold gift, a gift of knowledge and a gift of power. President Brigham Young explained that as we participate in temple ordinances, we are given the knowledge necessary to enable us to "walk back to the presence of the Father" (*Journal of Discourses,* 2:31). As we participate in and are taught by temple ordinances, we also have the opportunity to make covenants. When we keep the covenants we make in the temple, we receive the gift of power to put our knowledge to use. It is one thing to know how to do something; it is quite another to have the power to do it. Thus to lay claim to the temple endowment, to this marvelous gift of both knowledge and power, we must not only participate in temple worship but also keep the covenants we make there. Isaiah's latter-day vision of the people from the nations going to the temple suggests that they understood this truth, for he seems to have heard them say among themselves, "Come ye, and let us go up to the mountain of the Lord, to the house of the God of Jacob; and he will teach us of his ways and we will walk in his paths" (2:3). So it is for those of us who participate in temple worship today. As we learn of "his ways" we obtain the gift of knowledge. As we "walk in his paths" we obtain the gift of power. It is a paradigm that applies in all periods of time.

QUESTIONS TO PONDER

1. What four things, outlined in 2:4, will lead to millennial peace? Can any of these be achieved before the Millennium? How?

2. What are some modern versions of the sins denounced in 2:6–9?

Chapter 3

"THE DAUGHTERS OF ZION"

ISAIAH 3

A prophecy of famine accompanied by a dearth of leadership opens Isaiah 3. One fulfillment of this prophecy came during the Babylonian conquest of Jerusalem. When the Babylonians, weary of Judah's rebellion against their empire, took Jerusalem by siege (ca. 606 B.C.), they apparently carried away much of the promising leadership and talent, leaving "the poorest sort of the people in the land" (2 Kings 24:14). They eventually appointed Zedekiah to be a vassal king over the remnant left in Judah, but when he proved as rebellious as his predecessors, they besieged Jerusalem again and carried away most of the remaining people (ca. 587 B.C.). Famine, as described by Isaiah, naturally accompanied the sieges of Jerusalem (3:1, 7). And the deportation of their rulers left them with children, as well as reluctant men and women, to lead them (3:2–7, 12). Couched in this prophecy is the warning that these things will befall Judah for their wickedness, especially for their pride, lack of compassion, and cruelty to one another (3:5, 9–11, 15–17).

A prophecy directed towards the daughters of Zion concludes Isaiah 3. Through Isaiah the Lord chastises these daughters for their flirtatious ways (3:16) and warns that all the superficial and outward adornments in which they have invested will be taken away, leaving them pitifully unattractive, repulsive, and desolate (3:17–26).

LIKENING ISAIAH'S WORDS UNTO OURSELVES

The metaphor of the Lord Jehovah as the bridegroom and the covenant people as the bride espoused or married to Him is found throughout the prophetic writings of the Old Testament. The imagery is powerful. It suggests that the love, devotion, faith, and trust that should exist between God and His covenant people should be as deep and enduring as that which should exist between a husband and wife.

The prophecy of the daughters of Zion can be understood as an example of this bride and bridegroom metaphor. Like all good daughters of Isaiah's day and culture, the espoused (covenant) people should have been keeping themselves pure and virtuous, awaiting the day when they would meet their bridegroom (Christ). But instead, this worldly people are doing just the opposite: "The daughters of Zion are haughty, and walk with stretched forth necks and wanton eyes, walking and mincing as they go, and making a tinkling with their feet" (3:16). Rather than virtuously preparing for marriage, these unfaithful daughters are prostituting themselves. Far from seeking beauty in purity and devotion, they bedeck themselves in all manner of worldly adornments to attract other lovers (3:18–23). Rather than maintaining the faith and fidelity requisite to finding everlasting joy through the Lord's covenant, they are wantonly seeking for pleasure in promiscuity and self-indulgence.

Isaiah warns that all the temporal, vain, and worldly adornments with which the promiscuous daughters of Zion hope to beautify themselves in an effort to attract adulterous (idolatrous) lovers, and all the effort they put into trying to find happiness outside of God's plan for eternal happiness, will ultimately pass away unfulfilled (3:18–24). "And it shall come to pass, that instead of sweet smell there shall be stink; and instead of a girdle a rent; and instead of well set hair baldness; and instead of a stomacher a girding of sackcloth; and burning instead of beauty" (3:24). In their humbled and contemptible state, they will sit at the gates of the city and weep, but to no avail, for the lovers they sought will have fallen "by the sword" (3:25), and those remaining will not take these foul and filthy daughters, regardless of what they have to offer (4:1). Every evil thing in which they trust and hope to find pleasure will be lost or turned against them. Instead of finding happiness, they can expect to find abandonment, captivity, desolation, and humiliation.

God wants us to be happy and has a wonderful plan for our eternal joy, but He will not allow his children to find happiness in sin. Lasting joy is found only in faithfully doing our God's will.

QUESTIONS TO PONDER

1. What mistakes lead to the pitiful conditions described in 3:1–15? (consider especially 3:5, 14, 15). What can we learn from their mistakes?

2. In what situations would the message contained in 3:16–26 help a teenager? How could the principles be taught to young children?

Chapter 4

"THE BRANCH OF THE LORD"

ISAIAH 4

The prophecy concerning the daughters of Zion that concludes Isaiah 3 is continued into the first verse of Isaiah 4, but the subject of the prophecy changes in verse 2. Rather than speaking of the wicked and apostate daughters, the prophet addresses those who remain faithful, calling them the "branch of the Lord" (4:2). Rather than being repulsively smelly, torn-girdled, bald, and scabby headed (3:17, 24), this righteous branch of the daughters who remain after the Lord purges and washes away the filth of wickedness are "beautiful and glorious" and enjoy the presence and protection of the Lord (4:2).

LIKENING ISAIAH'S WORDS UNTO OURSELVES

We can find hope, courage, and comfort in knowing that it is possible to remain a faithful "branch of the Lord," even while living in a very wicked world. Isaiah describes those who stay faithful under such conditions as "them that are escaped" (4:2), perhaps meaning that they have not been caught up or led astray by the adversary. They are free, because they are not taken captive by sin. The Lord promises that such will find a "tabernacle for a shadow in the daytime from the heat, and for a place of refuge, and for a covert from storm and from rain" (4:6). In a world full of evil, hatred, and turmoil, we can indeed find refuge in the tabernacle of our faith.

QUESTIONS TO PONDER

1. How do you suppose the Lord washes and purges us as described in 4:4?

2. How does one become a "branch of the Lord described" in 4:2–6?

3. How can we make the Lord and His plan our refuge from the storm as described in 4:5–6?

Chapter 5

"WHAT COULD HAVE BEEN DONE MORE TO MY VINEYARD?"

ISAIAH 5

In Isaiah's day the annual grape harvest in the Holy Land was a time of great celebration, for grapes and the wine made from them were an essential part of both the economy and the sustenance of the people. Harvest songs were part of the work and the celebration. As Isaiah 5 opens, the prophet appears to be using such a harvest song to teach the people about their relationship with God and His efforts to bless them. In this song of the vineyard, Isaiah likens the covenant people to the grapevines and the Lord to the husbandman who plants and cares for them (5:1–7).

After the song of the vineyard, Isaiah denounces particular sins he sees among the people and outlines some of the consequences for them. He warns that the land mongers who hoard land to enrich themselves will find the land unproductive (5:8–10). He rebukes the hedonists who drink and party all day and night, warning that they will end up thirsty, famished, humbled, and forsaken (5:11–17). He pronounces woe upon those who love sin (5:18), who seek signs (5:19), who call evil good and good evil (5:20), who are proud of their own intellects

(5:21), who are drunkards (5:22), and who love money more than justice (5:23). All such, Isaiah prophesies, incur the wrath of God and will be destroyed (5:24–25).

The chapter ends with a prophecy of the Lord lifting up an ensign to those he calls to punish his wicked people. They will speedily come, without weariness. They will rush in like an invading army on horses and chariots, roaring like lions as they lay hold of their prey and carry them away. Many scholars see this as a prophecy of the Assyrian conquest and deportation of Israel that occurred around 727 B.C.

LIKENING ISAIAH'S WORDS UNTO OURSELVES

The climate and soil in the Holy Land are ideal for growing grapes—so ideal that grapes even grow wild, though the fruit wild grapevines produce is far inferior to the plump, sweet, and juicy fruit produced by cultivated plants. With a little timely and skilled pruning, cultivating, and fertilizing, the grape clusters grow large and heavy. The keeper of the vineyard in Isaiah's song did everything requisite to produce such a harvest. He planted it in an ideal location, a "very fruitful hill" (5:1). He "fenced it, and gathered out the stones thereof, and planted it with the choicest vine"—not just any vines (Hebrew, "*gephen*") but rather with the very best (Hebrew, "*sorek*"). He "built a tower in the midst of it" to protect it "and also made a winepress therein" (5:2). Normally a winepress would be hewn out of the native rock and that single winepress would serve an entire community of vineyards, but the keeper was anticipating such an abundant harvest from his special care that he made one just for this vineyard and placed it therein.

Imagine the disappointment of the keeper of the vineyard when, rather than bringing forth delicious fruit, it produces "wild grapes" (5:2), a phrase the King James translators used to translate the Hebrew term *beushim*, which literally means "worthless stinking things." You can feel the keeper's frustration as he laments: "And now, O inhabitants of Jerusalem, and men of Judah, judge, I pray you, betwixt me and my vineyard. What could have been done more to my vineyard, that I have not done in it?" (5:3–4).

With such a disappointing result from his labors, a typical farmer would likely plow the vineyard under or set fire to the vines. But this keeper does not respond in either of those ways. Instead, through his actions we learn something about how God deals with us when we do not respond appropriately to His loving care and nurture: "And now go to; I will tell you what I will do to my vineyard: I will take away the hedge thereof, and it shall be eaten up; and break down the wall thereof, and it shall be trodden down: and I will lay it waste: it shall not be pruned, nor digged; but there shall come up briers and thorns: I will also command the clouds that they rain no rain upon it" (5:5–6). It appears that rather than immediately destroying the vines, the keeper of the vineyard leaves them to struggle on their own.

Something similar happens in our own lives when we make evil choices or ignore the promptings of the Holy Spirit. The Spirit withdraws for a season, and we are left to face the natural consequences of our choices. Our Heavenly Father, our Keeper, understands well the principle of tough love. He knows that in giving us the gift of agency, which is vital to His plan for our happiness, we have the choice to reject His blessings and teachings. He knows also that agency entails not only the right to choose but also the right to experience the consequences of our choices, for only then can we learn and grow—as painful as such consequences may sometimes be for us and for Him. It is a wonderful blessing to know that if we repent as we so learn, the Spirit will return to guide us, and God will continue to nurture and help us. If we are willing to respond to His blessing and care, God will help us grow to reach our fullest potential.

QUESTIONS TO PONDER

1. What could the grapes in 5:1–6 represent?

2. What kind of nurturing have you received from the Lord of the vineyard?

3. What kind of harvest are you bringing forth?

Chapter 6

"BUT THEY UNDERSTOOD NOT"

ISAIAH 6

Often referred to as Isaiah's call, Isaiah 6 chronicles a personal encounter the prophet had with the Lord and describes his experience. Isaiah informs us that this vision occurred in the year that King Uzziah died (ca. 740 B.C.; 6:1). The prophet tells of seeing the Lord sitting in power and glory upon His throne in the temple, surrounded by ministering seraphim (6:2–4). He describes his feelings of unworthiness at being in the Lord's presence until a seraph cleanses his lips with a coal from the altar (6:5–7). He recounts his willingness to respond to the Lord's call, "Whom shall I send?" by declaring, "Here am I; send me" (6:8). Isaiah then shares the counsel and instruction the Lord gave him as he accepted the call (6:9–10) as well as the response the Lord gave to his inquiry about how long he was to minister (6:11–12). The vision closed with the Lord's assurance that though the covenant people would be forsaken and scattered, a tithe (tenth), or remnant, would eventually return.

LIKENING ISAIAH'S WORDS UNTO OURSELVES

Verses 9 and 10 of Isaiah 6, especially as they are translated in the King James Version, are enigmatic: "And he said, Go, and tell this people, Hear ye indeed, but understand not; and see ye indeed, but perceive not. Make the heart of this people fat, and make their ears heavy, and shut their eyes; lest they see with their eyes, and hear with their ears, and understand with their heart, and convert, and be healed" (6:9–10).

Upon first reading, the language of this passage appears to suggest that the Lord is commanding Isaiah to preach to the people in a way that will confuse and bore them so they will not understand, repent, and be converted. Some who struggle to understand Isaiah may conclude that the prophet followed that commandment very well! The Book of Mormon text, however, which relies on a more ancient and more nearly original version of Isaiah than does the King James Version, makes an important clarification. It reads, "Go and tell this people—Hear ye indeed, but they understood not; and see ye indeed, but they perceived not" (2 Nephi 16:9). Thus, the Book of Mormon version of this verse helps us understand that the Lord is not telling Isaiah to confuse the people but rather informing him that they will choose to reject his words. Moreover, the Hebrew verb translated as "be healed" in the King James Version of verse 10 can also be translated, and perhaps is better translated, as "heal themselves." This alternative translation suggests that as the people reject Isaiah's words, they also reject the healing power of Christ's Atonement, choosing rather to try to heal themselves, perhaps through the works of the law and their own righteousness, as Paul later warned (for example, Romans 10:1–4).

Apparently, the purpose of the Lord's counsel to Isaiah as he accepts the call is to forewarn him that he will experience considerable rejection in his ministry. It appears that the Lord wants Isaiah to understand that his success in the ministry is not to be measured by how many people accept his message. If acceptance were the standard of success, then Isaiah and many other great prophets, such as Jeremiah, Abinadi, and even Christ would have to be classified as failures. But they were not. Perhaps Isaiah later recalled and found some comfort in this merciful forewarning as he faced the discouragement that accompanies rejection. The counsel can be helpful to modern missionaries as well. Real success should not be measured by the number of baptisms one performs but rather by how diligently one has labored to do the will of the Lord.

QUESTIONS TO PONDER

1. What elements of Isaiah's experience of being called as a prophet are similar to that of such other prophets as Ezekiel, John the Revelator, Lehi, and Joseph Smith?

2. How is Isaiah a type for Christ in 6:8? (see also Abraham 3:27).

3. What does Isaiah's example teach us about accepting callings?

Chapter 7

"CALL HIS NAME IMMANUEL"

ISAIAH 7

In the eighth century before Christ, Assyria was building its empire by conquering neighboring nations and making them vassal states. When the kingdoms of Israel and Syria were subdued by the Assyrians, they formed a military alliance in the hope of winning their independence. Pekah, king of Israel, and Rezin, king of Syria, invited Ahaz, king of Judah, to join with them, but Ahaz refused. Because of that refusal, Syria and Israel planned to attack their sister nation of Judah. They wanted to remove Ahaz and put their own man on the throne, the son of Tabeal, apparently thinking that the son of Tabeal would then join their alliance against Assyria. It is in this historical context that the events of Isaiah 7 occurred.

The Lord sent Isaiah and his son to deliver a message to King Ahaz, informing him that Syria and Ephraim (the name Isaiah often uses to refer to the kingdom of Israel) would not succeed in conquering Judah and removing Ahaz as king (7:1–7). The prophet promised Ahaz that within sixty-five years Ephraim would cease to be a nation; this prophecy was fulfilled about 721 B.C. when Assyria gathered up and carried away the rebellious

29

kingdom of Israel (7:8–9). Remarkably, Isaiah then invited
Ahaz to ask for a sign to verify that the message he shared with
him was indeed from God. Feigning piety, Ahaz refused Isaiah's
offer. Perhaps this was because he had already determined to
make an alliance with Assyria to protect himself from the Syria-
Israel threat, despite the Lord's warning through His prophet
(7:10–12; compare 2 Kings 16:7–20). Isaiah saw through the
wicked king's hypocrisy (7:13) and informed Ahaz that the Lord
would give him a sign anyway, even Immanuel (7:14–16). Isaiah
then warned Ahaz of the consequences Judah would face if he
trusted in Assyria for deliverance rather than trusting in the
Lord. The prophet described the military invasion and enslave-
ment Judah would suffer for the folly (7:17–20), as well as the
socioeconomic consequences they would pay as they were forced
back into being primitive pastoralists (7:21–25).

LIKENING ISAIAH'S WORDS UNTO OURSELVES

The Immanuel prophecy was given to Ahaz as a sign to convince him that Isaiah was speaking for the Lord. The King James
Translation reads, "Behold, a virgin shall conceive, and bear a
son, and shall call his name Immanuel" (7:14). *Immanuel* means
"God is with us." Isaiah further explained to Ahaz that "before
the child [Immanuel] shall know to refuse the evil, and choose
the good" the kings of Israel and Syria would no longer be a
threat (7:16).

Latter-day Saints typically understand this to be a wonderful
prophecy of the virgin birth of Christ, but if so, many wonder
how a prophecy concerning the birth of Christ could be a useful
sign to Ahaz when he lived more than seven hundred years before Jesus was born. Most faithful scholars and students resolve
the issue by concluding that the prophecy refers not only to the

birth of Jesus Christ but also to a son of Isaiah (for example, *Maher-shalal-hash-baz;* 8:1, 3), or Ahaz, or some other person, soon to be born to a young woman who lived during Isaiah's day. The Hebrew term translated in this passage as "virgin" can refer not just to a woman who has never known a man, such as Mary, the mother of Jesus, but also to any young woman of child-bearing age. Perhaps the sign to Ahaz was that a young woman then living would conceive and bear a son and before that child would reach an age of accountability, the threat to Judah of the Syria-Israel alliance would be gone. The birth of the child was thus a sign of deliverance, that God was with his people—Immanuel—to save them.

Even though Isaiah's son Maher-shalal-hash-baz, or some other child to be born in Ahaz's day, may indeed have been a fulfillment of this prophecy, that child must be viewed as a type, or foreshadowing, of Jesus, for only He could rightfully bear the title "Immanuel." The name precisely describes Jesus of Nazareth, born to the virgin Mary. He was more than just a good man in whom God put His Spirit, as some early Gnostics taught. He was more than just a wandering teacher among the Jews, as some modern historians conclude. Before He came to this earth, Jesus had attained the stature of a God. He was the great Jehovah, divinely invested with the authority to speak and act in the name of the Father, the God of Abraham, Isaac, and Jacob, the God who created the earth, spoke to Moses, parted the Red Sea, and brought down the walls of Jericho. Upon His birth He set that power and stature aside. He condescended to take on mortality, to be born as a weak and dependent infant in the humblest of circumstances to a peasant couple living in an obscure corner of the world. He literally became "God with us," that He might save us from sin and death.

QUESTIONS TO PONDER

1. What "signs" has the Lord given in your life that demonstrate that God is with you?

2. What could ancient Assyria represent in modern times?

Chapter 8

A SANCTUARY OR
A STONE OF STUMBLING

ISAIAh 8

L ike the previous chapter, Isaiah 8 admonishes the covenant
people to trust in the Lord rather than in alliances with
other nations. The chapter opens with instructions for Isaiah to
give his newborn son the name of Maher-shalal-hash-baz, which
is a combination of Hebrew terms meaning to quickly and excit-
edly spoil and take prey. This child, much like Immanuel, was
to be a sign to the covenant people that the destruction of Syria
and Israel was imminent (8:1–4; compare 7:14–16).

Through Isaiah the Lord warns that because the people refuse to trust Him and His covenant, symbolized by the gentle
waters of Shiloah, He will send upon them a very different kind
of water, even the decimating deluge of Assyria that would over-
flow them and reach even to their neck (8:5–8). A fulfillment of
this prophecy occurred in 701 B.C. when Assyria invaded Judah
and conquered the region around Jerusalem, the head of the nation. The city of Jerusalem would also have fallen at that time
had not the faith of King Hezekiah and Isaiah allowed them to
access the powers of heaven and be delivered by divine intervention (36–37).

In plain words Isaiah warns the people that if they make confederacies or associations or counsel with other nations rather than trusting the Lord, they will be "broken" and "come to nought" (8:9–10). The prophet bears witness that he intends to wait upon the Lord and that he and his children are serving as signs and wonders sent from the Lord (8:17–18). He affirms his conviction that the people should look to God for direction and inspiration and warns that those who do not will find themselves forsaken, hungry, and in the dark (8:19–22).

LIKENING ISAIAH'S WORDS UNTO OURSELVES

There is a feeling both of tender pleading and of stern warning in Isaiah's admonition, "Sanctify the Lord of hosts himself; let him be your fear, and let him be your dread" (8:13). The prophet promises that if we fear, or reverence, the Lord, He will be a sanctuary for us. In times of adversity, suffering, or turmoil, those blessed with a testimony and an understanding of Jesus Christ can find peace, perspective, and hope in their faith—a refuge and a sanctuary from the storms of life. In contrast, those who have access to the covenants of the Lord and reject Him will find that the blessings offered them will become a "stone of stumbling" and a "rock of offence" (8:14). "For of him unto whom much is given much is required; and he who sins against the greater light shall receive the greater condemnation" (D&C 82:3). Such is the blessing and the burden of being a covenant people. Because we have the privilege of learning the gospel and making covenants with our Heavenly Father, we can lay claim to His greatest blessings or we can reap His greatest condemnation. Our privilege of faith in Christ can be a sanctuary or a stone of stumbling. The choice is ours—a choice manifested by how we live, love, serve, and obey.

QUESTIONS TO PONDER

1. How do we partake of "the waters of Shiloah" today? (8:6).

2. What does it mean to "wait upon the Lord"? (8:17).

Chapter 9

A GREAT LIGHT WILL SHINE INTO DARKNESS

ISAIAH 9

Isaiah 9 opens with one of the most beautiful messianic prophecies in the book of Isaiah. It likens the Messiah to a "great light" that will shine in the lands of Zebulun and Naphtali, which in the Savior's time were the areas around Nazareth and the Sea of Galilee (9:2). The prophecy promises that the Messiah will break the yoke, staff, and rod of the "oppressor" and ultimately reign in power and glory (9:6–8).

Following the wonderful Messianic promise, Isaiah turns his attention to the contemporary condition of the people. He rebukes them for their pride and warns that Syria and the Philistines will devour them (9:12). He chastises them for their widespread hypocrisy and evil doings and describes the equally widespread destruction they can expect (9:13–21). With each rebuke he assures the people that God's displeasure will last as long as they persist in iniquity. "For all this his anger is not turned away, but his hand is stretched out still" (9:21).

LIKENING ISAIAH'S WORDS UNTO OURSELVES

The lands of Zebulun and Naphtali about which the prophet speaks in the opening of Isaiah 9 are different from much of the rest of the Holy Land. A good part of the region, particularly around the Sea of Galilee, is covered in black basalt, unlike most of the Holy Land, which is blanketed in light-colored limestone. Anciently, houses in the region were built primarily from this black igneous stone, giving them a dark appearance both inside and out. It could be said that the people living there walked in a land of "darkness." Moreover, because the region sat at the junction of important ancient roads through the Fertile Crescent, it was a primary military target, often conquered by invading forces. Consequently the occupants lived under the constant threat of attack, truly in the shadow of death. Isaiah seems to have these facts in mind when he declares, "The people that walked in darkness have seen a great light: they that dwell in the land of the shadow of death, upon them hath the light shined" (9:2).

If we understand that the great light is the mortal Messiah, then this prophecy presents two messages. First, in remarkable fashion, it tells us where Christ will minister—in the lands of Zebulun and Naphtali, among people that walked in darkness and dwelt in the land of the shadow of death. The lands include the area of Galilee where Jesus delivered most of His teachings and performed most of His public ministry. Such villages as Nazareth, Cana, Magdala, Capernaum, Chorazin, and Bethsaida, as well as the Mount of Beatitudes, the Sea of Galilee, and the Mount of Transfiguration, are all in this region. Second, in a spiritual sense, the prophecy beautifully describes what Christ would accomplish, for He would bring light to those who stumble in the darkness of error, sin, and apostasy, and He would bring hope to those who live in fear of death. Those who recognize and accept the Messiah's light will rejoice as He breaks the yoke, staff, and rod of the oppressor (9:3–4). That joy is felt by the faithful today as they find the deliverance from sin and hope for eternal life made available through the atoning sacrifice of Jesus Christ, He whom we recognize as "Wonderful, Counsellor, The Mighty God, The everlasting Father, The Prince of Peace" (9:6).

QUESTIONS TO PONDER

1. In what specific ways can we let the light of the Lord enter our lives?

2. What could the yoke, staff, and rod of 9:4 represent?

3. In what ways will Christ fulfill the titles given Him in 9:6?

Chapter 10

"SHALL THE AXE BOAST ITSELF?"

ISAIAᴎ 10

Isaiah 10 is the first in a series of prophecies the prophet gave concerning nations other than Israel and Judah. In this case, it is the most powerful military nation of Isaiah's day—Assyria. Continuing the theme of Isaiah 9, the first four verses of chapter 10 rebuke Israel and Judah for their unrighteousness, greed, and lack of charity, warning that there will be no place to flee when God visits them in His wrath. And even then, "For all this his anger is not turned away, but his hand is stretched out still" (10:4).

In the fifth verse, the Lord turns His attention specifically to Assyria, referring to the nation as "the rod of mine anger" whom He sent to chastise a "hypocritical nation," even the apostate covenant people (10:5–6). Assyria, however, failed to recognize God's hand in their rise to power but rather boasted in their own strength (10:7–14). Condemning them for their pride and arrogance, the Lord warns that ultimately Assyria will be decimated (10:16–19). The Lord then assures that a righteous remnant of Israel will survive the onslaught of Assyria and that through a mighty one (10:24–25), even an anointed one

(10:27), the burden afflicting the covenant people will be taken away and their enemies destroyed (10:20–34).

LIKENING ISAIAH'S WORDS UNTO OURSELVES

As the Lord condemns the boastful Assyrians for failing to recognize that they were but a tool He was using to discipline apostate Israel, He asks condemningly, "Shall the axe boast itself against him that heweth therewith?" (10:15). In their conceit and pride, the Assyrians had fallen into a trap that has snared humankind in every age and estranged them from their Maker. They failed to see the influence of God in their lives. They did not seek the will of the Lord and thus could not comprehend it. They did not understand their role in God's eternal plans and thus arrogantly concluded that everything they accomplished was done by their own power and genius. They did not understand that "in nothing doth man offend God, or against none is his wrath kindled, save those who confess not his hand in all things, and obey not his commandments" (D&C 59:21).

Like Assyria, those who commit such a spiritual blunder eventually find themselves left to their own power and genius, ultimately falling far short of what God could make of them and with them. They are a tool with great capacity, but because of their ignorance and lack of gratitude, they fail to qualify for divine help to access that capacity. They sit like an inanimate axe, with no "hewer" to help them accomplish the great work of which they are capable.

In contrast, if we gratefully recognize the Lord's hand in our lives and surrender our will to Him, asking Him to be the "hewer," to use us as He will, God can make something wonderful with us and of us. He can use us to accomplish His work and fashion us into exalted beings.

QUESTIONS TO PONDER

1. How does one become a humble tool in the hand of the Lord rather than a conceited axe?

2. How will the Lord remove the burden and destroy the yoke mentioned in 10:27?

Chapter 11

"AN ENSIGN FOR THE NATIONS"

ISAIAⱧ 11

Some of the most beautiful and familiar language describing the millennial reign of the Messiah opens Isaiah 11. Here we learn of the attributes and actions of Christ, the "stem of Jesse," when He comes in righteousness and power to destroy the wicked and usher in His wonderful theocracy of peace (11:1–9; compare D&C 113:1–2). The chapter closes with a prophecy of a great gathering and restoration of covenant people that is to occur before the coming of the millennial Messiah (11:10–16).

LIKENING ISAIAH'S WORDS UNTO OURSELVES

Latter-day Saints thrill at the promise of the closing verses of this prophecy. We are told that a root of Jesse will set up an ensign among the Gentiles, or the nations to which Gentiles and scattered Israel and Judah will gather and unite. Joseph Smith explained that this root of Jesse is a descendant of both Jesse and Joseph, who will hold the priesthood keys for the latter-day gathering of the covenant people (D&C 113:5–6). An ensign is a standard, or flag, to which people rally. The Hebrew term translated as "Gentiles" in verse 10 is translated as "nations" in verse 12. Thus the prophecy promises that in preparation for the millennial reign of the Messiah (11:1–9), a great latter-day leader will bring forth the restored gospel of Jesus Christ and gather the scattered covenant people.

Joseph Smith was such a latter-day leader. Through him God restored the gospel of Jesus Christ. To that gospel people from all nations are gathering and joining the great effort to bring back the "outcasts of Israel" and the "dispersed of Judah" (11:12) to the covenant, in preparation for the return of the Messiah. Latter-day Saints count it a privilege to be part of the preparation for the Lord's second coming.

QUESTIONS TO PONDER

1. What truths can be learned from the cause-and-effect relationship discussed in 11:9?

2. What is your own role in the prophecy given in 11:10–16?

Chapter 12

"WITH JOY SHALL YE DRAW WATER OUT OF THE WELLS OF SALVATION"

ISAIAH 12

The millennial return of Christ will be a time of great celebration and rejoicing for the righteous. In Isaiah 12 the prophet presents two songs of praise that will be sung by the faithful in the great time of peace ushered in by the second coming of Christ. It echoes the song of deliverance sung by Moses and the children of Israel at the parting of the Red Sea (Exodus 15:1–19) as well as the song of Deborah and Barak at the conquest of their enemies in the Valley of Jezreel (Judges 5).

LIKENING ISAIAH'S WORDS UNTO OURSELVES

The two hymns of praise in Isaiah 12 present a pattern that those blessed with the opportunity to accept the gospel should follow in any age. In the first song the millennial faithful express their testimonies (12:1–2). They sing their gratitude for the forgiveness and comfort God has granted them, declare their trust in Him, and testify that God is their salvation. In the second hymn, they encourage one another to share their joy and witness with others: "Declare his doings among the people, make mention that his name is exalted. . . . Cry out and shout, thou inhabitant of Zion: for great is the Holy One of Israel in the midst of thee" (12:4–6).

Each individual blessed with a testimony would do well to follow the pattern—to express faith and gratitude to God and to share the gospel with others. The promise to those so engaged is beautiful: "With joy shall ye draw water out of the wells of salvation" (12:3).

QUESTIONS TO PONDER

1. How do we draw from the wells of salvation described in 12:2–3?

2. How can a premillennial people sing these songs?

Chapter 13

"THE DAY OF THE LORD IS AT HAND"

ISAIAH 13

I n Isaiah's day the kingdom of Babylon was a center of culture, learning, and science. It was also a center for apostate religion, corruption, and sin. About a century after Isaiah's ministry, Babylon displaced Assyria as the dominant empire in the Fertile Crescent and inflicted suffering and captivity on its neighboring nations. Consequently, Babylon became a symbol, or type, for the world and its wickedness. The prophecy in Isaiah 13 anticipates Babylon's rise to power and foretells the reasons for and means of its subsequent destruction.

The opening verses describe the Lord's call to arms as He assembles a noble and righteous army to punish Babylon (13:1–5). The prophecy then describes the anguish, fear, and destruction that will accompany the punishment to be meted out upon Babylon in the day of the Lord (13:6–22). With vivid imagery Isaiah indicates that the devastation will occur not only from acts of war (13:15–18) but also from natural calamities and disasters (13:10, 13–14), leaving Babylon wasted and desolate, inhabited only by solitary creatures and wandering nomads (13:19–22). The middle verse of the prophecy identifies the iniquities of

Babylon that will incur the Lord's great wrath, including arrogance, pride, haughtiness, and tyranny (13:11). Remarkably, the prophecy identifies the Medes as one of the Lord's agents of destruction (13:17). This part of the prophecy was fulfilled near the end of the sixth century before Christ when King Cyrus, a Persian who conquered the Medes and added them to his forces, conquered Babylon.

LIKENING ISAIAH'S WORDS UNTO OURSELVES

As used by Isaiah, the phrase "day of the Lord" can mean any day in which the Lord punishes the wicked and rewards the righteous. The destruction of Babylon was a day of the Lord and can be viewed as a type for the great day of the Lord that will occur at the second coming of Christ. Thus this prophecy contains a vivid and accurate description of the downfall of Babylon that occurred in the sixth century before Christ and also describes the destruction of the worldly and wicked in the last days. It tells us that God will use forces on heaven and earth to punish and destroy the proud, the arrogant, the cruel, and the wicked (13:1–19). At the same time, we learn from the Book of Mormon text of Isaiah's prophecy that those who are faithful will find mercy and deliverance: We are assured that the Lord's "anger is not upon them that rejoice in [His] highness," and He "will be merciful unto [His] people, but the wicked shall perish" (2 Nephi 23:3, 22). Our latter-day challenge is to flee Babylon and live so that we may be numbered among those the Lord calls His "sanctified ones" (13:3).

QUESTIONS TO PONDER

1. Where do we fit into the prophecy given in 13:2–5?

2. What are we doing today to conquer spiritual Babylon?

Chapter 14

"I WILL BE LIKE THE MOST HIGH"

ISAIAH 14

I saiah 14:1–23 continues the prophecy of the fall of Babylon introduced in Isaiah 13. The first three verses promise that a gathering and restoration of the covenant people will coincide with the fall of Babylon. The Book of Mormon text of this prophecy is significantly different from that of the King James Version. The biblical text reads as if the strangers are to be servants to Israel, whereas the Book of Mormon text indicates that both Israel and the strangers will be servants of the Lord, thus clarifying that the covenant people will include both Israelites and righteous Gentiles, or strangers (2 Nephi 24:1–3; compare Isaiah 14:1–3).

Beginning in verse 4, the prophecy describes the fall of the king of Babylon (14:4–22). Isaiah recites a proverb that the people will speak against the defeated king (14:4–20). They will rejoice that the once-powerful tyrant who had caused so much misery among them has become weak and powerless (14:4–11). They ridicule him for his failed attempt to exalt himself at the expense of others (14:12–17). They delight that rather than enjoying a kingly burial, he is cast aside and trodden under foot

(14:18–20). The mocking of the fallen king is followed by the Lord's assurance that the children, or followers, of the despot will likewise be destroyed (14:21–23).

The chapter concludes with prophecies against two other traditional enemies of Israel—the Assyrians and the Philistines. It warns the Assyrians that the Lord intends to break them in His land and tread them under foot upon His mountain (14:24–28), a prophecy fulfilled in 701 B.C. and chronicled in Isaiah 36–37. The Philistines, or Palestina, are counseled not to rejoice when one oppressor passes away, for a more venomous one will follow (14:28–32), a prophecy that finds multiple fulfillments in history as one invading conqueror after another oppressed the land.

LIKENING ISAIAH'S WORDS UNTO OURSELVES

Just as the kingdom of Babylon is a type for worldliness and sin, so the king of Babylon can be viewed as a type for Satan. Latter-day Saints see in verses 12–14 doctrine fundamental to our faith. The plans of the king of Babylon to exalt himself at the expense of others echo Satan's primordial rebellion, wherein he sought to exalt himself above all others by denying them agency (Moses 4:1–4; 2 Nephi 2:17–18; D&C 29:36–37; 76:25–29). For he said in his heart, "I will ascend into heaven, I will exalt my throne above the stars of God: I will sit also upon the mount of the congregation, in the sides of the north: I will ascend above the heights of the clouds; I will be like the most High" (14:13–14).

He was Lucifer, meaning a "light bearer," and a son of the morning, yet in his greed for glory and power, he turned against the light. He wanted to be like the Most High, but in his conceit thought he alone should reach the goal. In his lust for power

Satan refused to recognize that the work and the glory of the Most High are to "bring to pass the immortality and eternal life of man" (Moses 1:39). Ironically, Satan wanted to bring to pass only the immortality and eternal life of himself and do it in a way that would thwart the very plan of God. Had Satan not rebelled, perhaps he would have realized that to truly be like the Most High, one should be involved in God's work and glory, helping others gain joy through eternal life rather than seeking to deny them the opportunity. Like so many selfish power-mongers in our modern world who subscribe to his philosophy, Lucifer did not comprehend the divine principle of servant leadership—that "he that is greatest among you shall be your servant" (Matthew 23:11).

How fortunate we are that One in the primordial council did understand the principle of servant leadership and was willing to serve and save us through His atoning sacrifice. Jesus Christ succeeded because He sought to do the will and the work of the Father. Like the Father, He sought the immortality and eternal life of man. How vital it is for us to remember that we too become more like the Most High as we serve others by teaching, helping, and assisting them in their efforts to follow God's "great plan of happiness" (Alma 42:8). As we help others gain their exaltation, we work out our own.

QUESTIONS TO PONDER

1. What responsibilities do Latter-day Saints have in bringing about the promises made in 14:1–2? (see 2 Nephi 24:1–2).

2. How do events described in 14:12–15 fit into God's plan of salvation?

3. What can we learn from 14:24 about the nature of God?

Chapter 15

"THEREFORE SHALL MOAB HOWL"

ISAIAH 15 and 16

In Isaiah 15 and 16 the prophet turns his attention to Moab. According to Genesis, the Moabites, whose country bordered the eastern side of the Dead Sea, were distant cousins of Israel through Lot (Genesis 19:30–38). Despite this relationship, the Israelites and Moabites were often hostile towards one another. Like the other small ancient kingdoms in the Fertile Crescent, Moab lived under constant threat of attack from the stronger, empire-building nations that preyed upon the region.

The prophecy begins with a detailed description and list of Moabite cities that will be taken by an invading force, likely the Assyrians (15:1–9). Isaiah knew Moabite geography well, for he lists cities to be conquered in Moab from east to west, and north to south, in the center of the country and out to the borders. The attack was to come in the night, suggesting that the people would be caught unawares and unprepared (15:1), leaving them to weep and mourn for the pillaging and destruction that accompanied their defeat.

Isaiah 16 focuses on the desperate attempts Moab will make to escape the invaders and find refuge in Judah. They will send lambs to Judah and plead with their estranged cousins to let their refugees dwell with them (16:1–5), but Judah will refuse their petition (16:6–8). Isaiah mourns the destruction that awaits Moab (16:9–11) and prophesies that all this will befall the kingdom within three years (16:12–14).

LIKENING ISAIAH'S WORDS UNTO OURSELVES

As Moab petitions Judah for refuge, the language turns messianic. Pleading for permission to let Moabite outcasts dwell with Judah and for Judah to protect them from the spoiler, Moab declares, "And in mercy shall the throne be established: and he shall sit upon it in truth in the tabernacle of David, judging, and seeking judgment, and hasting righteousness" (16:5). In this capacity Judah can indeed be viewed as a type for Christ, the One to whom we turn when we are in bondage or sin. Just as Moab sought deliverance from Judah, so do we look to Christ as our Savior.

Unfortunately, Moab historically had a hostile relationship with Judah rather than one of peace and trust. Consequently, Judah believed that Moab was not sincere in their desire to reconcile and refused to be their deliverer. Had Moab made peace with Judah before their hour of need, it is likely Judah would have come to their rescue. In a real sense Moab typifies those who attempt death-bed repentance—those who look to Christ only in times of desperate need. Moab might also be viewed as a type for those who practice the "sin now, pay later" way of life. Such misguided individuals reason that it is acceptable to live a wicked and sinful life now, for one can always repent later. Some may even plan when they will repent—perhaps just before they are to serve a mission or when they wish to marry in the house of the Lord. They fail to realize that such an attitude makes a mockery of the Savior's atoning sacrifice and demonstrates a lack of understanding and gratitude. Real repentance requires godly sorrow, a type of sorrow that cannot be simply turned on and off at a whim. Those who sin with impunity, thinking that repentance is an easy balm they can salve over their spiritual wounds when the time for their planned repentance arrives, will find it difficult if not impossible to muster the godly sorrow sufficient for forgiveness in their hour of need. Like Moab, they will find their sincerity questioned and their petition denied. "Therefore shall Moab howl" (16:7).

What a blessing to know that if we work throughout our lives to build a relationship of love, devotion, trust, and obedience with our Savior, then He will be our deliverer, our "shadow" and our "covert" (16:3–4). We will find that He is indeed a God of mercy who will come to our rescue to save and redeem us.

QUESTIONS TO PONDER

1. What can we learn about proper repentance from Moab's experience?

2. What is the difference between godly sorrow and howling?

Chapter 16

PLEASANT PLANTS AND STRANGE SLIPS

ISAIAH 17

During Isaiah's ministry the kingdom of Syria, whose capital was Damascus, formed a military alliance with the kingdom of Israel against the ravenous Assyrian empire. Isaiah 17 opens with a prophecy that, despite this alliance, both Syria and Israel (Ephraim) would be conquered (17:1–5). This prophecy of doom transitions into a prophecy of promise—the promise that although they would be conquered, a righteous remnant, likened to gleaning grapes and unharvested olives, would persist (17:6–7). Isaiah then describes the apostasy that would lead to God's forsaking of Israel and their ultimate defeat (17:9–11). As he closes the prophecy Isaiah warns the conquerors, even Assyria, the "rushing of mighty waters" (17:12; compare 8:5–8), that though they may enjoy success for a season, they too will be rebuked and disappear, like "chaff" and a "rolling thing" (a tumbleweed type of plant) chased by the wind (17:13).

LIKENING ISAIAH'S WORDS UNTO OURSELVES

Isaiah likens Israel's apostasy to foolish farmers planting worthless crops they hope will produce an abundant harvest.

"Because thou hast forgotten the God of thy salvation, and hast not been mindful of the rock of thy strength, therefore shalt thou plant pleasant plants, and shalt set [their fields] with strange slips" (17:10). In this context "strange" means foreign, or outside the covenant. A slip is a twig or cutting used instead of seeds to grow new plants. Thus, as Israel forgot the Lord and worshipped false gods, they were planting "strange slips." At first they found the plants "pleasant," and it appeared as if the plants would indeed produce a crop for them. "In the day shalt thou make thy plant to grow, and in the morning shalt thou make thy seed to flourish," but, Isaiah warns, "the harvest shall be a heap in the day of grief and of desperate sorrow" (17:11). Though they may worship other gods and perhaps invest considerable effort in the practice, there will be no harvest of happiness in the end, only grief and sorrow.

Today too there are many "strange slips" that a covenant people can plant. We may devote too much of our time and resources to the pursuit of pleasure, perhaps more than we devote to God. We may decide that sin is pleasing. We may convince ourselves that there are better ways to find happiness than in doing God's will. If we should make such mistakes we are indeed planting "strange slips." We may think that such efforts and activities will yield a harvest of happiness, and perhaps for a season they will show the promise of pleasure. But ultimately, if we so deceive ourselves, all we will reap is missed opportunity and sorrow. The hoped-for harvest will be a heap in the day of grief and desperate sorrow.

QUESTIONS TO PONDER

1. Who and where are "gleaning grapes" today? (17:6).

2. What are the strange slips that some cultivate in our time? (17:10–11).

3. What hope can a latter-day covenant people find in the prophecy given in 17:12–14?

Chapter 17

"HOW SHALL WE ESCAPE?"

ISAIAH 18 and 20

When Assyria began expanding south and west towards Egypt, adding Israel and then Judah to its empire as vassal states, Egypt sought to protect itself by offering to help Israel and Judah rebel against their overlords. The Egyptians hoped the ploy would keep Assyria occupied with putting down rebellion in Canaan so they would not be able to attack Egypt. Thus Egypt made many promises to send armies and resources to Israel and Judah if they would rebel—promises they did not intend to keep. Through Isaiah the Lord warned of Egypt's treachery.

Isaiah 18 is addressed to the "land shadowing with wings" that sends ambassadors in boats made of papyrus to a nation that has been scattered, trodden, and spoiled by the "rivers" (18:1–2). Scholars identify the shadowing land as Egypt, which sent emissaries to Judah and Israel, the nations trodden and scattered by Assyria, land of the rivers (compare 8:5–8; 17:12–14). In Isaiah's day, these ambassadors offered help and protection to Judah and Israel if they would foment the rebellion and war in Canaan that Egypt desired.

Isaiah passionately pleads with Israel and Judah to look to
the Lord for deliverance from their enemies at such times, rather
than looking for help from treacherous Egypt (for example, 18;
20; 30; 31). The prophet assures Israel and Judah that when
the battle flag is raised and the war horn sounded (18:3), just
when the enemies hope to harvest the spoil, the Lord will intervene to cut them down, leaving them to the beasts and the birds
(18:4–6). Isaiah prophesies that a remnant will then bring "the
present," or tribute, to the Lord in mount Zion (18:7).

To further emphasize the admonition, in 711 B.C., the year
that "Tartan came unto Ashdod" and "took it" (20:1), Isaiah
was instructed to walk naked and barefoot among the people
as a type, or sign, that the Egyptians and the Ethiopians too
would walk naked and barefoot as humiliated captives of Assyria
(20:2–5). With their promised protector, Egypt, conquered and
carried away, Judah would then wonder where they could turn
for protection from Assyria (20:6). The prophet's message dramatically made the point that not only would Egypt be unable
to protect Judah from Assyria but Egypt would not even be able
to protect itself. Isaiah hoped the prophecy would inspire Israel
to trust the Lord to be their deliverer rather than the self-serving
Egyptians.

LIKENING ISAIAH'S WORDS UNTO OURSELVES

In a sense the ancient Egyptians were a type for Satan. So
are entities in our own day who try to persuade us to trust in
them more than God in an effort to promote their own interests. A greedy businessman using deception to climb the corpo-
rate ladder, a wayward teenager trying to recruit others to join
in immoral activities, or a leader who feigns genuine concern to
win support for a self-promoting position might all be viewed as

modern versions of ancient Egypt. Their primary interest is their own selfish agenda. Like Egypt, they may try to convince others that they have a better plan for peace and happiness than that taught by God's prophet. With no regard for their own integrity or the welfare of others, they may deceptively make many promises they will not—and, in fact, cannot—keep. When the time comes for them to deliver on their promises, they are nowhere to be found. "And thus we see that the devil will not support his children" (Alma 30:60). Those who trust in such selfish entities may alienate themselves from God, especially if supporting such entities requires them to disregard God's commandments and the warnings of His prophet. Like Judah they may find themselves without divine support in their desperate hour, asking, "Whither we flee for help . . . and how shall we escape?" (20:6).

Although there are modern versions of ancient Egypt, it is a blessing to live in a time when the gospel has been restored so that we have prophets, teachers, and leaders to help us place our faith in God and warn us of entities and ideas that would turn us from Him. As we listen and learn from those who lovingly and genuinely care about our welfare and eternal happiness, we can find confidence, deliverance, and peace.

QUESTIONS TO PONDER

1. How can we recognize and not be deceived by those who, like ancient Egypt, seek to promote their own interests above all else?

2. How can we help them reform?

Chapter 18

"THEY SHALL RETURN EVEN TO THE LORD"

ISAIAH 19

Isaiah's prophecies often contain remarkable details. The "burden of Egypt" (19:1) is one example. Egypt was already an ancient civilization by Isaiah's day. For centuries it had been a world power militarily, economically, intellectually, and culturally. Yet the prophecy recorded in Isaiah 19 foretells a startling collapse of the nation. It speaks of civil war and unrest (19:2–3). It forewarns of oppressive rulers (19:4) and describes devastating ecological, financial, and social upheaval that will come as the river is dried up (19:4–16). It foretells a time when mighty Egypt will fear lowly Judah (19:17) and then describes a remarkable day when the Egyptians will be healed. In that day a savior will deliver smitten Egypt, and Egypt, Assyria, and Israel will be one in their devotion to the Lord (19:18–25).

LIKENING ISAIAH'S WORDS UNTO OURSELVES

Much of the prophecy recorded in Isaiah 19 must have sounded absurd to Isaiah's contemporaries. The description of civil war and oppressive kings in Egypt would have been believable enough, for those had already occurred in the land

(19:2–4), but that the river, which in Egypt could only have meant the mighty Nile, would be dried up, wasted, and turned far away would have been unfathomable (19:5–6). Likewise, the environmental demise and economic collapse described by Isaiah would have sounded incredible to the ears of his contemporary audience, as would the notion that Egypt would ever find tiny Judah to be a "terror" (19:17).

Yet today, with historical hindsight, we can see how these prophecies became a reality. The Aswan Dam, which was completed in 1970, turned the Nile River far away and ended its annual inundation. The unanticipated ecological impact of the dam brought about many of the subsequent consequences the prophecy foretells. Plants and animals that depended on the river's flow and regular flooding to maintain their habitat and sustain their life cycles were decimated. Consequently, farmers, fishers, and other businesses and industries that were tied to the productivity of the land failed. Rather than being an economic blessing to the nation, the dam has proven to be a disaster, making the "princes" and "counsellors" who constructed the dam appear foolish (19:11). Likewise, Judah did indeed become a "terror" unto Egypt (19:17) as in 1948, 1956, 1967, and 1973 the newly created nation of Israel fought and won wars against that once-mighty nation.

While the fulfillment of the portions of this prophecy that are historical to us are easy to understand, the portions that are still in our future may seem unbelievable, perhaps as unbelievable to us as the Nile being dried up and Judah ever being a terror to Egypt would have seemed to Isaiah's contemporaries. It may be difficult for us today to imagine a time when Israelites and non-Israelites will embrace the gospel in peace and unity. Still, the reality that what once would have sounded incredible

to the people of Isaiah's time is now a fact should give us hope
that God will provide a way to bring about the peace and righteousness foretold in this prophecy—even if it now seems so far
away and impossible. "For with God nothing shall be impossible" (Luke 1:37).

QUESTIONS TO PONDER

1. What can we learn from Isaiah 19 about the nature and purpose of prophecy?

2. How do you envision your part in the fulfillment of the
   prophecy given in 19:18–25?

Chapter 19

"BABYLON IS FALLEN, IS FALLEN"

ISAIAH 21

In Isaiah 21 the prophet again turns his attention to Babylon, the "burden of the desert of the sea" (21:1). Isaiah saw the destruction of Babylon in a vision and was deeply pained by the grievous devastation (21:2–4). He set a watchman to look for the fulfillment of the vision, which eventually is reported by a messenger declaring, "Babylon is fallen, is fallen" (21:5–10). Isaiah closes the prophecy by foretelling the similar destruction of such smaller nations and peoples as Dumah, Dedanim, Tema, and Arabia, which bordered on or had some other connection with Israel and Judah (21:11–17).

LIKENING ISAIAH'S WORDS UNTO OURSELVES

That Isaiah would be pained by the destruction of an enemy (21:2–4) would surprise some in our time who do not follow the Savior's admonition to "love your enemies, bless them that curse you, do good to them that hate you, and pray for them which despitefully use you, and persecute you" (Matthew 5:44). The anguish Isaiah feels for the suffering of others, whether friend or foe, is a window to the greatness of his soul and an example for those in our dispensation who are striving to become like Christ.

QUESTIONS TO PONDER

1. When and how do you think spiritual Babylon will fall? Will it be a process? An event? Will it be public? Individual?

2. Why do you think God spoke about the small countries and peoples listed at the end of Isaiah 21?

Chapter 20

"THEY SHALL HANG UPON HIM ALL THE GLORY"

ISAIAH 22

The prophecy in Isaiah 22 opens with a disturbing vision. Isaiah sees the people in Jerusalem reveling on their rooftops and is moved to weep for them, for he knows that they will soon be under siege by an invading nation (22:1–7). He describes the desperate measures they will take to defend themselves (22:8–11) but warns that they will be conquered and carried away for their worldliness and iniquities (22:12–14). The prophet is then sent to Shebna, a government official who typifies the apostate covenant people. Isaiah chastises Shebna for occupying himself with building a richly adorned sepulcher on earth at the expense of doing God's will and warns that the wayward leader will be removed from his position and carried away to die in another country (22:15–19). Isaiah informs Shebna that he will be replaced by a man named Eliakim, a man who will bring glory to his father's house (22:20–25).

LIKENING ISAIAH'S WORDS UNTO OURSELVES

Eliakim is a remarkable type for Christ. His name can be interpreted as "my God shall arise," or "my God shall cause to arise." Both of these interpretations point to Christ, for He arose from the dead and He brought to pass the resurrection of all, causing all to arise and live again. The "key of the house of David" was placed upon Christ (22:22), and He brought glory to His Father and His Father's house when He was fastened as a nail in a sure place—a striking image that points to His crucifixion (22:22–23). Fastened as a nail in a sure place, Christ bore the sins and burdens, the "vessels of flagons" of the children of His Father, the "offspring and the issue" (22:23–24). Ultimately the nail would be removed and the burdens lifted (22:25). As our beloved hymn assures, "Once all things he meekly bore, / But he now will bear no more" (*Hymns,* no. 196). As children of our Heavenly Father, our hope for glory hangs upon Him whom we love as our Savior.

QUESTIONS TO PONDER

1. How could a covenant people become as oblivious to physical and spiritual danger as Judah had become? (22:1–19).

2. How can we avoid the pitfalls and condemnation of Shebna? (22:15–19).

3. How do we hang vessels upon our Savior? (22:22–24).

Chapter 21

"HOLINESS TO THE LORD"

ISAIAH 23

Isaiah 23 concludes the writings sometimes referred to as the prophecies to other nations (10–23). Although these chapters also contain prophecies to Judah and Israel (for example, 11; 12; 17; 22), Isaiah focuses much of his attention on other nations, including the major powers of Isaiah's day, Assyria (10), Babylon (13–14; 21) and Egypt (19–20), as well as nations bordering the promised land, such as Moab (15–16) and Syria (17). In chapter 23 Isaiah speaks to yet another bordering nation, Phoenicia. The prophecy describes how the once prosperous Phoenician merchant city of Tyre will be laid waste, leaving all those who traded in her seaport to mourn and howl over her destruction (23:1–14). The prophecy speaks of a seventy-year respite for the forsaken city, followed by its return to wealth and sin and ultimately its designation as "holiness to the Lord" (23:18), in this context likely meaning consecrated for destruction (24:18).

LIKENING ISAIAH'S WORDS UNTO OURSELVES

The ancient Near East was typically polytheistic, with every nation having its own patron deities. Thus, nations contemporary with Isaiah could have variously worshipped the Philistine god Dagon, the Canaanite Baal or the Babylonian Marduk, to name a few. By prophesying to other nations, Isaiah not only kept Israel and Judah informed about what the Lord had in store for their neighbors but also gave the message that, in truth, Jehovah is God over all nations. Similarly, humankind today has many differing views of the reality, nature, and numbers of deity. How fortunate we are in this dispensation to know that there is a living prophet who, like Isaiah of old, declares God is real. He is our Creator and the God of all the earth. Though modern versions of Tyre, Babylon, and Assyria may fail to recognize Him, He is still their God. Truth stands, whether it is accepted or not.

QUESTIONS TO PONDER

1. Why did Tyre return to her evil ways? (23:15–18).

2. How can we avoid the same folly?

Chapter 22

"THE EARTH IS DEFILED UNDER THE INHABITANTS THEREOF"

ISAIAH 24

Isaiah 24 through 35 are sometimes called Isaiah's apocalypse because they reveal events in the last days of this earth, alternately describing the terrible destruction of the wicked and the blessing and rejoicing of the righteous as they welcome the Messiah and His millennial theocracy of peace. Isaiah 24 begins the apocalypse, graphically describing the sorrow and suffering of the wicked in the opening and closing verses (24:1–12, 16–23). The middle of the chapter describes the joy of the righteous remnant who, rather than fearing and suffering at that time, "sing for the majesty of the Lord" (24:14).

LIKENING ISAIAH'S WORDS UNTO OURSELVES

Isaiah explains that the apocalyptic destruction will come because "the earth is defiled under the inhabitants thereof" (24:5). He describes three ways the wicked in the latter days defile the earth: "They have transgressed the laws, changed the ordinance" and "broken the everlasting covenant" (24:5). It is not difficult to imagine what disturbing things Isaiah saw in our time under each of those headings. Perhaps as he decried the transgression of the law he witnessed the impunity with which so many in modern societies violate the law of chastity, the observance of the Sabbath, or the principle of integrity. It is likely he saw how some in this generation have altered or discounted such sacred ordinances as baptism, marriage, and the sacrament. Perhaps most disconcerting to Isaiah was the breaking of the "everlasting covenant" (24:5).

Adam was given the very covenant Isaiah references in this prophecy. Later it became known as the Abrahamic covenant. The New Testament calls it the "everlasting covenant" (Hebrews 13:20). In our day it is sometimes called "a new and an everlasting covenant" (for example, D&C 22:1; 132:4, 6).

Expressed simply, the covenant promises that if we follow Heavenly Father's plan, we can become like Him. The everlasting covenant includes many principles and ordinances, such as the new and everlasting covenant of marriage and the new and everlasting covenant of baptism. In some periods of history some aspects of the covenant have varied. For example, in Abraham's day the covenant included ordinances of circumcision and blood sacrifice. In our dispensation it includes the ordinance of the sacrament. Despite these slight differences, the promise of the covenant has been consistent in all ages. If we follow God's plan, we can become as He is.

Perhaps Isaiah saw those in our time who declare that it is impossible and, in fact, blasphemous to teach that we can become like our Heavenly Father. Imagine how the prophet felt about those in our day who declare God's covenant an "unchristian" doctrine. He would certainly have concluded that those who deem the idea that we can become like God a heresy have themselves broken the "everlasting" covenant and rendered mortality meaningless.

Latter-day Saints understand that the primary purpose of mortality is to abide by the covenant, to follow God's plan and become like Him. We believe God when He commanded us to be perfect, even as He is perfect (Matthew 5:48). We honestly believe that when God gives such a commandment He prepares a means for us to follow it (1 Nephi 3:7). We call that means whereby we become like our Heavenly Father the plan of salvation or the plan of happiness. We rejoice that the plan provides a way for us to grow through the exercise of agency and faith. We are humbled and grateful that the plan also includes a Redeemer to rescue us from sin and death. We have the assurance that as we keep this covenant and abide by its ordinances and laws, the earth will be sanctified for us, rather than defiled by us. Rather than fearing our God, we will feel to "sing for the majesty of the Lord" (24:14).

QUESTIONS TO PONDER

1. By what criteria will the Lord's punishment be meted out, according to 24:2? Will we be protected?

2. What is the opposite of defiling the earth as described in 24:5? How can we accomplish it?

Chapter 23

"WINES ON THE LEES
WELL REFINED"

ISAIAH 25

Isaiah 25 continues the prophet's apocalypse with a song, or psalm, of praise to be sung by the faithful during the Messiah's reign (compare Isaiah 12). The psalm praises the Lord for destroying the wicked, even the "city of the terrible nations" (25:3). It reverences Him for strengthening, nurturing, and protecting the faithful poor and needy (25:4). With beautiful imagery the psalm describes the celebratory "feast of fat things" to be held "in this mountain," or Zion (25:6; compare D&C 58:8–12; Revelation 19:9–10, 17–18), again reminding us of temple worship (compare Isaiah 2), as the Lord removes the "covering" that is "cast over all people" (25:6; compare 2 Corinthians 3:14). Tender language testifies that the Lord will "swallow up death in victory" and "wipe away tears from off all faces" (25:8). Those privileged to join in this beautiful hymn will testify, "Lo, this is our God; we have waited for him, and he will save us: this is the Lord; we have waited for him, we will be glad and rejoice in his salvation" (25:9).

LIKENING ISAIAH'S WORDS UNTO OURSELVES

As Isaiah describes the gathering of the faithful to Zion, he indicates that they will partake of "wines on the lees well refined" (25:6). In the process of making wine, "lees" are the sediments of yeast and pulp that settle to the bottom of the wine vat during processing, after the grapes have been trampled. Some types of wine sit upon the lees for a time to improve their flavor and quality; others will be ruined if they are left upon the lees. Thus, lees can be understood as a type, or symbol, of things that can make us better or worse, depending on what we are made of. Trials and challenges can be lees. They can help us grow and even sanctify us (D&C 101:3–5), or they can leave us bitter and angry, depending on our character and faith.

In the context of Isaiah 25, where "wines on the lees" are offered in the Lord's mountain, lees can also be likened to temple covenants. As we enter the mountain of the Lord's house we have the privilege of making sacred covenants. If we live true to those covenants, then the covenants enrich our lives and prepare us for exaltation. If we violate those covenants, however, we become a poor wine that is made worse for sitting on the lees. Temple covenants can qualify us for God's greatest blessings or His greatest condemnations, depending on what we are made of.

QUESTIONS TO PONDER

1. What determines the type of wine we are? (25:6). How do we change?

2. How does the Lord "swallow up death in victory" for us? (25:8).

Chapter 24

"AWAKE AND SING, YE THAT DWELL IN THE DUST"

ISAIAH 26

Isaiah 26 opens with a song of praise, faith, and trust that will be sung by the righteous who witness the coming of the Messiah (26:1–9). This prophetic psalm further observes that while the wicked do not learn righteousness when the Lord shows them favor (26:10–11, 16–18), the faithful who have waited for Him and confessed their devotion to Him will find peace, prosperity, protection, and restoration (26:8, 12–15, 19–21).

LIKENING ISAIAH'S WORDS UNTO OURSELVES

As the faithful sing their devotion to Jehovah in this psalm they declare, "O Lord our God, other lords beside thee have had dominion over us; but by thee only will we make mention of thy name. They are dead, they shall not live; they are deceased, they shall not rise" (26:13–14). The Hebrew term translated "Lord" in this passage is the sacred name *YHWH* and always refers to Jehovah. On the other hand, the term translated "lords" is *adonim* in Hebrew and refers generically to masters, rulers, or, as is likely in this context, other gods. According to the mythology, the Canaanite god Baal, to which Israel often apostatized, would die and rise from the dead every year, as did some of the other gods in the Canaanite pantheon. The words of this psalm sung by Jehovah's faithful appear to be a polemic or argument against the worship of Baal. They declare that there is in truth only one God, Jehovah, who will cause the false gods' "memory to perish" (26:14). Despite the mythology, those gods are dead. The psalm assures us that they do not and will not rise from the grave (26:14). This observation is in stark contrast to Jehovah's promise later in the passage that the time will come when He truly will rise from the grave and the dead will join Him in the resurrection. "Thy dead men shall live, together with my dead body shall they arise. Awake and sing, ye that dwell in dust: for thy dew is as the dew of herbs, and the earth shall cast out the dead" (26:19). Thus this beautiful psalm testifies and prophesies that Jehovah will take on mortality and die and rise from the tomb, thereby giving us the gift of resurrection.

QUESTIONS TO PONDER

1. What does it mean to keep our mind stayed on the Lord? What is the promise associated with doing so? (26:3).

2. What could be the favor mentioned in 26:10? How do we learn from it?

Chapter 25

"YE SHALL BE GATHERED ONE BY ONE"

ISAIAH 27

Isaiah 27 begins "In that day," referring to the day when Messiah restores His people and reigns on the earth, the day the Lord will slay "the dragon that is in the sea" (27:1).

Another millennial psalm (compare Isaiah 25–26) follows this prophecy, but in this case Jehovah is the voice rather than His people. The psalm uses imagery similar to the song of the vineyard in Isaiah 5:1–6, which likens Israel to a vineyard. But in this case, rather than bringing forth wild grapes, the vineyard nurtured by Jehovah will "blossom and bud, and fill the face of the world with fruit" (27:6). The enemies of the vineyard, those "who would set briers and thorns against" it, will be destroyed—or, if they wish, they can choose to make peace with the Lord by taking hold of His strength (27:4).

Following Jehovah's psalm a series of rhetorical questions teaches how the Lord will chastise the rebellious of Israel. The Lord asks the people to consider if He deals with the covenant people in the same fashion He deals with their enemies (27:7). Answering His own question, the Lord observes that in some measure He does indeed but that He "stayeth his rough wind in the day of the east wind" (27:8). An east wind is a dry, destructive wind. Thus the Lord appears to be saying that although He does indeed punish the rebellious of the covenant people, the punishment is measured. He does not afflict them excessively with a rough wind when they are facing an east wind, and through this careful and appropriate chastening "shall the iniquity of Jacob be purged" (27:9).

In typical apocalyptic fashion, this prophecy of destruction for the wicked is followed with a note of hope as the Lord promises that the righteous will be saved and gathered to worship "in the holy mount" (27:13).

LIKENING ISAIAH'S WORDS UNTO OURSELVES

"The Lord shall beat off [thresh] from the channel of the river unto the stream of Egypt, and ye shall be gathered one by one, O ye children of Israel" (27:12). The harvest imagery Isaiah uses promises that the Lord will go from one end of the earth to the other as He gathers, or threshes out, the scattered, lost, and outcast of the children of Israel—one at a time. Latter-day Saints understand how this careful harvesting of individuals will be accomplished. Using similar imagery, the Lord told the Prophet Joseph Smith in 1829 that the latter-day "field is white already to harvest; and lo, he that thrusteth in his sickle with his might, the same layeth up in store that he perisheth not, but bringeth salvation to his soul" (D&C 4:4). Since that prophetic declaration was written, thousands upon thousands of missionaries have traveled throughout the world to declare that the gospel of Jesus Christ has been restored to the earth. These missionaries have understood that they are part of the Lord's great work to find and restore His covenant people. Lesson by lesson, testimony by testimony, family by family, one by one scattered Israel is being sought, found, and taught by the Lord's harvesters.

QUESTIONS TO PONDER

1. What can we learn about agency and the Lord's feelings for His children in His counsel in 27:4–6 to those who set briers and thorns?

2. What are the metaphorical similarities between our missionary efforts and harvest labor?

Chapter 26

"THIS ALSO COMETH FROM THE LORD"

ISAIAH 28

At the beginning of Isaiah 28 the prophet again warns proud and drunken Ephraim, the kingdom of Israel, of the mighty Assyrian flood that is about to come upon them (28:1–4; compare 8:6–8). Again, the destruction wrought by the Assyrians serves as a type for the destruction of the wicked in the last days. In typical contrasting apocalyptic fashion the prophet anticipates the glory and beauty that will define the subsequent millennial reign of the Messiah (28:5–6). He then chastises the rulers of Ephraim who in their drunken state wallow in their own filth and vomit (28:7–8). Those rulers in turn appear to mock the prophet, accusing him of trying to teach them like small, just-weaned children, "precept upon precept," "line upon line," "here a little, and there a little" (28:9–11). With deadly condemnation, Isaiah turns the inebriated rulers' mocking complaint upon its ear, assuring them that the word of God is indeed given "precept upon precept," "line upon line," "here a little, and there a little," and that their refusal to hear would cause them to "fall backward, and be broken, and snared, and taken" (28:12–13).

Isaiah further condemns the alliance, or "covenant with death," that the kingdoms of Judah and Israel were making with other nations to defend themselves, assuring them that such alliances would fail when the Lord arises to punish them (28:14–22; compare Isaiah 7–8). The warning portends a future time when "scornful" rulers in Jerusalem would make a "covenant with death" to kill the mortal Messiah, only to see that "covenant . . . disannulled" when the "sure foundation" and "precious corner stone" rose from the tomb (28:14–18; compare John 11:47–53; 20:1–31).

The chapter closes with a fascinating and inspirational agricultural metaphor designed to teach how the Lord cultivates His children during mortality (28:23–29).

LIKENING ISAIAH'S WORDS UNTO OURSELVES

The complex metaphor that concludes this chapter teaches principles fundamental to our faith. It begins with a rhetorical question: "Doth the plowman plow all day to sow?" (28:24). In other words, Isaiah asks if a plowman plows the same field over and over again? The answer, of course, is no. Rather, "when he hath made plain [level] the face thereof" and broken the clods of the ground (28:24–25), he begins to sow various kinds of seeds in different ways.

First he plants "fitches" and "cumin" (28:25). Fitches are likely a plant commonly known today as nutmeg flower. This plant grows on a delicate stem to about twelve inches tall. It has a white or pale blue flower that matures into a walnut-sized seed pod. The pod is very brittle and loaded with tiny seeds that are valued as a pungent spice. The cumin mentioned in this verse is likely the same plant as our modern cumin. This member of the carrot family grows one or two feet tall and produces clusters of white to pink flowers which, at maturity, yield the spicy seeds that are used in kitchens today. Both fitches and cumin have relatively tiny seeds that do not require special spacing in their planting, so the wise farmer plants these seeds by merely casting them abroad—by throwing (*zaraq*) and scattering (*hephitz*) them over the ground. Today we would call this type of planting broadcast seeding. When seeds are sown by broadcasting they grow close together in dense patches or clusters, which happens to be an ideal condition for fitches and cumin, for if the plants are sown too widely apart they do not compete as well with other vegetation. But when planted close together in tight communities, fitches and cumin thrive, creating their own microenvironment that preserves moisture and chokes out competing weeds.

Next, the farmer plants three kinds of cereal grains. First he will "cast in the principal wheat." Bread wheat is the most important food crop grown anciently and today. It is truly the staff of life. Accordingly, this critical crop is planted with special care. The Hebrew term *sowrah,* translated here as "principal," is better translated as "in rows." Thus, rather than merely throwing out the seeds, the wise farmer "casts" (from the Hebrew *sam,* meaning to put or place) the seeds in rows. By carefully placing the seeds in rows, the farmer assures that his precious wheat crop will have adequate spacing for the irrigation, cultivation, and ripening it needs to thrive.

After the wheat the farmer plants the "appointed barley," a term better translated as "barley in the appointed place." Barley is a grain inferior to wheat for human consumption. Barley bread is the poor man's bread. The redeeming value of barley is that it will grow in places where wheat will not. It is much more tolerant of poor soils, especially saline soils. If a farmer has a portion of his field with poor drainage, which causes the salinity of the soil to increase, that portion becomes the appointed place for barley. The farmer knows that while precious wheat may not grow there, barley will do just fine.

Finally the farmer plants the "rie." The Hebrew term translated here as "in its place," *gebulto,* is better translated as "on the edges or borders." Thus the farmer plants the rie around the edges of his field, perhaps to form a living hedge or fence to protect the other crops. The rie planted here is likely referring to a type of spelt wheat that is not free threshing, meaning the seeds cannot be easily separated from the seed heads. This kind of wheat is a poor grain for human use and is more commonly used for animal fodder and straw and, in this case, as a protective hedge.

From the description we can visualize the farmer's field. In one portion he has a nicely broadcast patch of fitches and in another a broadcast patch of cumin. In the choicest part of his field he has carefully placed rows of wheat. In the poorest sections of the field he has planted barley and then surrounded the entire field with a protective hedge of rie.

To understand this metaphor it is helpful to liken the farmer to our Heavenly Father and the seeds to ourselves. We sometimes wonder why we are born where and when we were. Is the time and place of our birth capricious? Latter-day Saints believe the answer is no. Fundamental to our faith is the understanding that before we came to this earth, we lived in a premortal existence with a loving Heavenly Father. We further understand that in that premortal state we had agency and that we grew and developed as we used that agency. Some, as Abraham learned, became noble and great ones (Abraham 3:22–23). We believe that when it came time for us to experience mortality, a loving

Heavenly Father, who knows each of us well, sent us to earth at the time and place and in the circumstances that would best help us reach our divine potential and help Him maximize His harvest of redeemed souls. Some of us are fitches and cumin. We are born and raised in tight knit and supportive communities and are a vital and contributing part. Others of us are wheat. We have been placed in exceptionally fertile and promising places because God knows our special potential and is counting on us to produce so much. Some of us are barley and rie. We have been placed in difficult circumstances, perhaps having to face handicaps and hardships, but God knows us. He knows our needs, our hearts, and our abilities, and knows we can reach our divine potential, even in the face of great trials. Perhaps these very trials will help us reach our potential, or perhaps He allows us to face those trials so we can help others reach theirs as well.

The teaching in this passage does not end with the planting of the seeds but continues through to the harvest. Isaiah observes that "fitches are not threshed with a threshing instrument, neither is a cart wheel turned about upon the cumin" (28:27). The threshing instrument mentioned here is known today as a threshing sled. This toboggan-shaped tool is typically about six feet long and two to three feet wide. On the underside of the sled, rocks or pieces of flint or obsidian are embedded. Anciently and in some places still today, when a farmer is harvesting his grain he will cut it close to the ground, tie it into sheaves, and then place the sheaves on an area of hard-beaten earth called a threshing floor. When the threshing floor is covered with sheaves, he will place the threshing sled on top of the sheaves, weigh it down with something, and then have it pulled around over the sheaves. As the threshing sled is pulled over the sheaves, the kernels of grain are knocked out of the seed heads, and the rest of the plant is chopped into chaff. Then on a windy day the farmer will use his winnowing fork to toss the mixture of chaff and grain into the air. As he does so, the lighter chaff is blown away, leaving the clean kernels of grain behind. In the absence of a threshing sled the farmer may use a heavy cart to thresh the grain.

But Isaiah observes that threshing sleds and carts are not used on fitches and cumin. Knowing something about the plants makes the reason obvious. Fitches and cumin are too delicate and their seeds too tiny to withstand the rigors of a threshing sled or the weight of a cart. Using such implements would grind the seeds into oblivion. Rather, Isaiah observes, "fitches are beaten out with a staff, and the cummin with a rod" (28:27). Likely the farmer places a piece of cloth on the ground and then, while holding the plants over it, lightly taps the seed heads with a stick. As he does so the fragile seed heads break open and spill their contents onto the cloth. All it takes is a little light tapping with a stick. But imagine what would happen if we tried to thresh wheat in this manner. You could spend an entire day lightly tapping the seed heads and have very little to show for your labors. The wise farmer knows that wheat and other cereals need to be vigorously and rigorously threshed to get the harvest from them. As Isaiah explained, "Bread corn is bruised; because he will not ever be threshing it" (28:28).

Perhaps the threshing refers to the challenges and trials we experience in life that, if properly processed, bring out the best in each of us. Or perhaps the threshing represents opportunities, talents, and callings we are given. Thus some of us are like fitches and cumin—it takes only a little nudge or challenge, and the goodness just spills out. Others of us more likely resemble wheat. We have to be vigorously pushed and challenged before our potential surfaces. The point is that God knows us and loves us, and if we will trust Him and involve Him in our lives, then He will see that we have the challenges and opportunities—the threshing—that will help us realize our fullest potential.

QUESTIONS TO PONDER

1. How can the precepts and lines the Lord teaches be both a blessing and a condemnation in our lives? (28:9–13).

2. How can the prophecy in 28:14–18 be understood as messianic? How do events recorded in John 11:47–57 inform the interpretation?

3. What kind of plant do you most identify with in 28:23–29? How can a person change?

Chapter 27

"A BOOK THAT IS SEALED"

ISAIAH 29

Latter-day Saints love Isaiah 29 from Nephi's use of it to prophesy the coming forth of the Book of Mormon (2 Nephi 27). The original prophecy in Isaiah is directed to "Ariel," the "city where David dwelt," which is commonly understood to be Jerusalem (29:1). It foretells a time when Jerusalem will experience invasion, siege, disasters, and conquest, leaving its inhabitants to whisper from the grave like one who communicates with the dead through a necromancer, or familiar spirit (29:2–6). It further prophesies that the nations who fight against Jerusalem will not be satiated by their conquests and will eventually pass away like chaff (29:5, 7–8).

The prophecy then speaks of a time Latter-day Saints typically understand to be the Apostasy, a time when men spiritually stagger as if inebriated or in a deep sleep, for they have rejected the prophets, seers, and rulers (29:9–10; see also 2 Nephi 27:1–5). The books are sealed to them, and when the books are delivered cannot be read by them (see Joseph Smith–History 1:63–65; 2 Nephi 27:15–20). The apostates teach the precepts of men, and the desires of their hearts do not match the words of their lips (29:11–13). In response to such apostasy, we are told, God will intervene to perform a "marvellous work and a wonder" that will vanquish and expose the foolish who think themselves prudent, who suppose that they can hide their thoughts and activities from God and who seek to discount or explain away the work of God (29:14).

This great work will change the people's values. The forests of Lebanon, a symbol of pride and arrogance (for example, 2:13) will be replaced by fruitful fields, a symbol of righteous covenant people (29:17; see also, for example, 5:1–7; 27:2–6). The deaf will hear the "words of the book" that is to play a role in God's marvelous work, and the blind will be given vision (29:18). They will sanctify God's name, and those who erred will learn truth, while the scornful and conspirators will be brought to nought (29:20–24).

Nephi saw his own people and the future restoration of the gospel in the new promised land as a fulfillment of this prophecy. He foresaw a time of apostasy among the Gentiles who would inhabit the land in the latter days (2 Nephi 27:1–5). He recognized the Book of Mormon, the record of his own people, as the sealed book that would come forth by the power of Christ and be read upon the housetops like a voice out of the dust as part of the marvelous work (2 Nephi 27:6–11). He knew of the three witnesses who would testify to the truth of the book (2 Nephi 27:12–13). He foresaw the learned men who would struggle to read the book and the unlearned Joseph Smith who would do so by the power of God (2 Nephi 27:15–22; see also Joseph Smith–History 1:63–65). He understood how the book would expose evil and restore truth (2 Nephi 27: 26–35).

LIKENING ISAIAH'S WORDS UNTO OURSELVES

According to Jeremiah, it was the law and custom in his day to make two copies of a business transaction or agreement, one sealed and the other left open to the public (Jeremiah 32:9–15). Apparently business was conducted according to the terms of the open document, but if the open document was ever lost or destroyed or if there was suspicion that it had been altered, then the sealed document was opened and used to restore the terms of the original agreement. The sealed document might also contain additional information meant only for those involved in the transaction and not for public use.

The practice as outlined in Jeremiah can help us better understand the purpose of the Book of Mormon and the timing of its coming forth. God's dealings with humankind, His covenants, were recorded in both the Bible and the Book of Mormon. For centuries, the Bible was the open copy of the covenant, available for public use. Unfortunately, through the process of time and by the designs of conspiring men, parts of it were lost and others altered, leaving many who wanted to understand their relationship with God and their obligations to Him confused and misinformed, causing them to stumble spiritually (1 Nephi 13:23–29). When the time was right, God brought forth the sealed copy of the covenant, the Book of Mormon, through the Prophet Joseph Smith to restore the fulness and truth of His covenant, His gospel.

Isaiah understood the vital role of the Book of Mormon in bringing greater understanding and truth to our day. Latter-day Saints understand that the Book of Mormon has the power to transform our lives and bring individuals to Christ. It is a blessing and a responsibility for us to share the teachings and doctrines, the terms and covenants of the part of the "sealed book" now available to us to help our Heavenly Father in His marvelous work to restore truth and redeem His children.

QUESTIONS TO PONDER

1. What do events foretold in Isaiah 29 reveal about the relationship between man's agency and God's plans?

2. Both condemnation and blessings seem to accompany the marvelous work described in 29:14–24. What makes the difference?

Chapter 28

"THIS IS THE WAY, WALK YE IN IT"

ISAIAH 30

In the opening verses of Isaiah 30, the prophet again admonishes Israel and Judah against making alliances with Egypt to protect themselves from their enemies (30:1–2; compare Isaiah 13; 20; 31). Isaiah warns of the shame and failure that will accompany such an alliance (30:3–7). He then chastises the people for rejecting the Lord's prophets and seers and for despising their teachings, trusting in their alliances and their own strength for deliverance rather than God (30:8–11, 15–17). With vivid imagery Isaiah describes the defeat the people will experience for their rebellion, warning that they are a "breach ready to fall," that they will be broken like the "potters' vessel," and that "one thousand shall flee at the rebuke of one" (30:13–14, 17).

The prophecy then turns from one of warning and rebuke to one of hope and encouragement. Isaiah assures the people that the Lord is gracious, merciful, patient, and willing to answer their cries (30:18–19). Though He gives them the bread of adversity and the water of affliction when they are disobedient, yet He will give them righteous teachers to show them the way and will bless them abundantly with prosperity, productivity, and light as they repent (30:20–26).

In the closing verses of the chapter Isaiah returns to his apocalyptic theme, foretelling the ultimate victory of the Lord. He speaks again of the indignation of the Lord that will devour the evil, sift the nations, beat down the Assyrians, and kindle the burning of those ordained for destruction, while the faithful will celebrate His victory with song and gladness of heart (30:27–33).

LIKENING ISAIAH'S WORDS UNTO OURSELVES

One great challenge parents face is knowing when and how to apply tough love—when to discipline children or allow them to experience the consequences of their choices—and how to follow up on the discipline, once it is administered. Three principles for guiding such decisions can be found in Isaiah's description of the discipline God administers to His children. First, through the prophet God carefully and clearly explains the choices His children have. They can make alliances with and trust in Egypt to protect them, or they can listen to God's prophets, sit still, return, be confident, and wait for the deliverance the Lord promises them (30:7, 15, 18). Second, God carefully and clearly explains the consequences they can expect for their decisions. If they decide trusting Egypt is their best option, they will be shamefully conquered and forced to flee, but if they trust in the Lord, they will continue to dwell in Jerusalem and enjoy light and prosperity (30:3–19, 23–26). Finally, God makes certain that even if His children make wrong choices and have to suffer the bread of adversity for their foolishness, He does not give up on them but rather continues to provide teachers to encourage His children, "This is the way, walk ye in it" (30:21).

QUESTIONS TO PONDER

1. How can we follow the counsel in 30:15?

2. What kinds of bread and water can we receive from the Lord? (30:20; compare John 4, 6).

Chapter 29

"THEIR HORSES ARE FLESH"

ISAIAⱧ 31

I saiah 31 is the last of a series of chapters warning Israel and Judah against trusting in Egypt for deliverance or protection from Assyria (compare 18; 20; 30). Isaiah warns that though the Egyptian military resources may appear formidable, if the people choose to turn to Egypt for help rather than to the Lord, then "both he that helpeth" and "he that is holpen" will fall (31:3). The prophet then encourages the people to trust in God by assuring them that the Lord will fight for mount Zion and will defend and deliver Jerusalem (31:4–5). He promises Israel and Judah that as they turn unto God and put away their idols, the Assyrians will fall and flee back to their homes in fear, a promise realized as chronicled in Isaiah 36 and 37 (31:6–9).

LIKENING ISAIAH'S WORDS UNTO OURSELVES

Isaiah emphasizes the great contrast between the omnipotence of our eternal God and the impotence of mortals and all that is temporal when he reasons, "Now the Egyptians are men, and not God; and their horses flesh, and not spirit" (31:3). The point is poignant. Why would any reasonable people place their hopes for deliverance in the feeble hands of man when they have access to the blessings and protection of the Almighty? Why would they trust the arm of flesh at the expense of divine succor? Many today are willing to settle for the puny protection and transitory treasures of the temporal—what we can see and feel right now—rather than letting our faith grant us access to the power of God and the riches of eternity. We settle for horses of flesh rather than chariots of fire. Wise parents, counselors, and friends would do well to remind those they love who find themselves tempted to ignore the heavens and settle for the things of the world that such horses are flesh.

QUESTIONS TO PONDER

1. How could the principles taught in this chapter help a teenager being tempted by peers to compromise standards?

2. What does the imperative "turn" in 31:6 mean for us?

Chapter 30

"RISE UP, YE WOMEN THAT ARE AT EASE"

ISAIAH 32

A description of the millennial reign of the king Messiah opens Isaiah 32. We learn that He "shall reign in righteousness," lead and protect His people, change the values and perspectives of humankind, and expose the wicked (32:1–8). The chapter closes with a beautiful portrayal of a faithful covenant people living in peace and prosperity (32:15–20). These prophecies of hope bracket a warning and rebuke given to the covenant people who are at ease, here symbolized as women without care. They are admonished to hear the voice of God and cease being complacent, for famine and desolation await them (32:9–14). By placing this warning in the middle of the passage, the prophet emphasizes that the promised blessings of peace and prosperity are not intended for those who are at ease or careless.

LIKENING ISAIAH'S WORDS UNTO OURSELVES

The Hebrew term translated "careless" in this passage means to be unconcerned, casual, or complacent. It is the opposite of being engaged, aware, and valiant. Just as Isaiah was concerned about the complacency of the covenant people in his day, so

Nephi warned that in the last days Satan will "pacify" and "lull" many into a sense of "carnal security," convincing them that "all is well in Zion," and thus cheat their souls and lead them "carefully down to hell" (2 Nephi 28:20–21). There is irony in Satan "carefully" leading the "careless." In a revelation given through the Prophet Joseph Smith, we learn that those who are careless, those who are not valiant in the testimony of Christ, will find themselves in a kingdom less than celestial (D&C 76:71–80).

Thus we understand that if those who have access to the blessings of the gospel take them for granted, if they become casual or thoughtless in the way they obey, pray, serve, worship, or care for others, then not only do they become easy prey to the designs of the devil but they also forfeit eternal blessings and the opportunity to become like our Heavenly Father. How fortunate we are that our God is not careless—He is not casual, lackadaisical, or unconcerned as He goes about His work and glory.

Through Isaiah the Lord presents a simple formula for avoiding the pitfall of complacency. He admonishes us to "hear [His] voice," and "give ear unto [His] speech" (32:9–11). We are blessed to have many ways to hear God's voice. We hear it when we sincerely pray, when we carefully study the scriptures, when we listen to the teachings of living prophets, and when we recognize the promptings of the Holy Ghost. As we diligently and regularly seek for and listen to God's voice through these marvelous resources, feelings come into our hearts and thoughts come into our minds that tell us how we can become more Christlike. We find ourselves troubled about the things we should be troubled about and encouraged to make ourselves better. As we discipline ourselves to act upon those thoughts and feelings, the conduit of communication between ourselves and God grows closer and clearer. We find ourselves anxiously engaged in following God's great plan for our eternal happiness and in helping others do so as well. We become "Latter-day Saints" rather than "Latter-day Ain'ts."

QUESTIONS TO PONDER

1. How can we recognize carelessness in our lives?

2. What are we going to do to prevent it?

Chapter 31

"WHO AMONG US
SHALL DWELL?"

ISAIAᵬ 33

*T*he prophet returns to an apocalyptic theme in Isaiah 33. He begins by warning the spoilers and those who deal treacherously that they will in turn be spoiled and destroyed when the Lord rises and fills Zion with judgment and righteousness (33:1–13). Isaiah closes the chapter with a poetic description of what the Lord's coming will mean to the faithful, who will see the king in his beauty, and enjoy peace and prosperity (33:16–24). He notes that in the theocracy Christ will establish, the Savior will administer every branch of government, foretelling the day when "the Lord is our judge, the Lord is our lawgiver, the Lord is our king; and he will save us" (33:22).

As is often his practice, Isaiah places the most poignant portion of his prophecy in the middle of the chapter. After he describes the fiery devastation that will consume the wicked (33:11–12), the prophet asks and answers the all-important question, "Who among us shall dwell with the devouring fire?" (33:14).

LIKENING ISAIAH'S WORDS UNTO OURSELVES

Those who "wait" for the Lord (33:2) in anticipation of enjoying the millennial blessings promised in Isaiah 33:16–24 are especially interested in Isaiah's description of who among us shall dwell with Christ at His second coming. The prophet lists characteristics of those who will dwell in millennial joy: "He that walketh righteously, and speaketh uprightly; he that despiseth the gain of oppressions, that shaketh his hands from holding of bribes, that stoppeth his ears from hearing of blood, and shutteth his eyes from seeing evil" (33:15).

Reviewing the list leads us to conclude that Isaiah was well aware of spiritual maladies that would afflict our day. The list provides a paradigm for conducting a self-evaluation of our spiritual health and our readiness to meet our God. Consider the following questions:

Do I walk righteously? Am I sincerely striving to think, feel, say, and do the things my heart tells me God would have me think, feel, say, and do?

Do I speak uprightly? Are my words and actions congruent with the will of the Lord and in harmony with it? In today's vernacular, do I walk the walk and talk the talk? Am I willing to teach of my faith? Am I willing to share my testimony? Am I vocal in defending that which is right?

Do I despise the gains of oppression and refuse to be influenced by bribes? Am I more concerned about the welfare of others than unfairly enriching myself at their expense? Is integrity more important to me than fame, power, or material wealth?

Do I stop my ears from "the hearing of blood" and my "eyes from seeing evil"? (33:15). Do I eschew violence and immorality? Do I avoid violent, immoral, and otherwise evil entertainment?

Am I careful not to entertain activities or thoughts that would profane the sacred powers to take and create life?

Isaiah teaches that if we can honestly answer yes to each of these questions, then we will see "the king in his beauty" and be blessed to have Him as our judge, our lawgiver, our king, and our Savior (33:17, 22).

QUESTIONS TO PONDER

1. In addition to being prepared for the coming of Christ, what blessings will we receive for living the type of life described in 33:15?

2. What is the best motivation for living such a life? What is our motivation?

3. Are you comfortable with the Lord acting as the executive, legislative, and judicial branch of millennial government as described in 33:22? Why?

Chapter 32

"NONE SHALL WANT HER MATE"

ISAIAH 34 and 35

Isaiah 34 and 35 conclude the section sometimes called Isaiah's Apocalypse (chapters 24–35) and provide a synopsis of the prophet's apocalyptic message. Isaiah 34 focuses primarily on the destruction of the wicked, graphically describing their slaughter and the ecological devastation that will accompany the day of the Lord's vengeance (34:1–10). Rather than being populated and prosperous, their land will be overrun with thorns, nettles, and brambles, a habitat suitable only for wild beasts, solitary birds, and scavengers (34:11–15).

In contrast, Isaiah 35 contains a euphoric description of the millennial blessings that await the faithful. Their land will become beautiful and productive (35:1–2, 6–7). The blind, deaf, and lame will be healed (35:5–6). The ransomed of the Lord will return to Zion with joy and peace, and sorrow and sighing shall flee away (35:8–10).

The final two verses of chapter 34 provide a bridge, or transition, between these two opposing fates of the people in that great day (34:16–17; compare JST 34:16). As is typical of Isaiah, these verses seem to be placed so the reader will identify in their teachings the point or principle the prophet most wants to emphasize. The verses speak of those whose names and works are recorded in "the book of the Lord" (34:16), assuring that such individuals can expect blessings rather than destruction when their God comes with both "vengeance" and "recompense" (35:4).

LIKENING ISAIAH'S WORDS UNTO OURSELVES

The promises given to those whose names and works are recorded in the book of the Lord (34:16, 17) lead us to ask, "What is the book of the Lord, and how do we get our name and works recorded therein?" In his apocalypse, John the Revelator spoke of books that record the works of humankind and out of which we will be judged (Revelation 20:12–15). A revelation given through the Prophet Joseph Smith to W. W. Phelps likewise speaks of books that record the names and works of individuals and that will be used to determine their eternal inheritances (D&C 85:6–11). In speaking of the importance of recording sacred ordinances, Joseph Smith further taught that whenever an ordinance is properly performed, witnessed, and recorded on earth, it is likewise recorded in heaven and that such records constitute the books out of which we will be judged (D&C 128:1–9). The book of the Lord of which Isaiah speaks appears to be such a record.

Latter-day Saints find great hope in the promises given to those whose names are written in this heavenly record, as well as Old Testament support for doctrines fundamental to our faith. We understand that if our names are in the book—that is to say, if we have had saving ordinances properly performed, witnessed, and recorded—then we are candidates to receive an eternal inheritance (34:17) that is to be enjoyed with our spouses

(34:16). Isaiah teaches that none who are in the book "shall want [lack] her mate," one of the earliest and clearest promises that God has provided a way for marriage to be eternal (34:16). As Latter-day Saints, we strive not only to have our names recorded in the book of the Lord but also to live true to the covenants and promises that we make in connection with sacred ordinances.

QUESTIONS TO PONDER

1. Isaiah describes a God of both vengeance and recompense in these chapters. Must He be both? Why?

2. Why are the joyful described in 35:10 as "ransomed"? Also in this verse, what does "return" mean for us?

Chapter 33

"BUT THEY HELD THEIR PEACE"

ISAIAH 36

The book of Isaiah is sometimes divided into three sections. Chapters 1–35 seem to be primarily prophecies of warning and judgment, with promises of deliverance, restoration, and redemption added as well. Chapters 40–66 are primarily chapters of deliverance, restoration, and redemption, with warnings and judgments added. Chapters 36–39 are a historical interlude, a case study of sorts that forms a bridge between these two principal sections. As these chapters chronicle the Assyrians' unsuccessful attempt to conquer righteous King Hezekiah, they provide a transition between destruction and deliverance. They illustrate how we can avoid the judgment and destruction of the first thirty-five chapters of Isaiah and lay claim to the deliverance and marvelous blessings promised in the last twenty-seven chapters (40–66) of the text.

Scattered throughout Isaiah's first thirty-five chapters are prophecies concerning the dreaded Assyrian empire. Isaiah knew that both Judah's alliance with Assyria and Israel's alliance against Assyria would end in disaster (7–8). He taught that Assyria was the "rod" of God's anger that He would use to

104

chastise His rebellious children (10:5). He warned that Assyria would invade Judah like a flood, reaching even up to its neck (8:6–8) but also promised that God would intervene to save Jerusalem (14:24–27; 17:12–14). He further promised that ultimately Assyria would be punished and destroyed for its arrogance and brutality (10).

Chapters 36 and 37 are historical chapters that report the fulfillment of some of these prophecies and warnings concerning Assyria. They tell of the Assyrian invasion of Judah in the days of righteous King Hezekiah and of God's intervention to save the people who supported their good king.

King Hezekiah had inherited Assyrian vassalage from his wicked father, Ahaz (7; 2 Kings 16:7–20). In 701 B.C. Assyria attacked Judah for Hezekiah's failure to pay in full the annual tribute they demanded. Initially the Assyrians swept through the nation conquering many cities. While attacking the city of Lachish, the Assyrian king, Sennacherib, sent his captain, Rabshakeh, to begin the siege of Jerusalem (36:1–3). The Assyrian captain hoped to intimidate the inhabitants of the city into panic and quick surrender. Standing outside the wall of the city he shouted threats to the people, warned that resistance would be futile, ridiculed their faith in Jehovah, mocked their defenses, and made empty promises if they would surrender (36:4–20). Had a wicked king ruled Jerusalem at the time, it likely would have fallen, as Isaiah foretold in chapter 22, but King Hezekiah trusted Jehovah and had inspired his people to do the same. Accordingly, the people followed Hezekiah's instructions and refused to respond to Rabshakeh's diatribe, holding their peace and answering him not a word (36:21–22).

LIKENING ISAIAH'S WORDS UNTO OURSELVES

Rabshakeh's vicious attempts to undermine the confidence of the faithful, to sow doubt in their minds, to put fear in their hearts, to shame them into surrender, are not unlike the tactics of some who attack our faith in God today. Whether it is open assailants challenging the doctrines of the Restoration or acquaintances ridiculing our commitment to the standards of the gospel, their motives and tactics frequently parallel the propaganda of the Assyrian captain. Too often truth and tolerance matter little to such individuals. They willingly sacrifice integrity on the altar of their ambitions.

While those who sincerely question or inquire about our faith or who are genuinely misinformed about our doctrine deserve a respectful and clear response from us, individuals who knowingly or purposefully distort the truth, who will not alter their attack or change their opinions in the light of truth, are often emboldened and encouraged by a rebuttal. When a response will only foster further contention, we may be wise to follow the example and admonition of King Hezekiah and his people. Sometimes the Spirit may direct that no answer is even better than a soft answer.

QUESTIONS TO PONDER

1. How can Isaiah 36 help us identify the Rabshakehs in our lives?

2. What is the fatal flaw in Rabshakeh's logic? (36:18–20).

Chapter 34

"INCLINE THINE EAR, O LORD, AND HEAR"

ISAIAH 37

The account of the Assyrian invasion of Judah in 701 B.C. continues in Isaiah 37. After listening to the threats and ridicule of Rabshakeh (36:4–20), Eliakim, Shebna, and Joah, King Hezekiah's representatives, rushed to report to him. The wise king rent his clothes as a sign of grief, went to the temple to petition the Lord, and sent his messengers to consult with Isaiah (37:1–5). The prophet counseled the men to fear not and made four prophecies in the name of the Lord concerning the fate of the king of Assyria (37:6–7):

1. God would send a blast, or plague, upon him;
2. The king would hear a rumor;
3. The king would return to his own land;
4. The king would fall by the sword in his own land.

The fulfillment of each of these prophecies is recorded in Isaiah 37. Following the conquest of Lachish, while attacking Libnah, Sennacherib, the Assyrian king, did indeed hear a rumor. He heard that Ethiopia was entering the war against him. Apparently fearing the consequences of having too many battlefronts, he sent a threatening letter to King Hezekiah, hoping to frighten the ruler of Judah into a quick surrender (37:8–13). King Hezekiah took the letter to the temple and spread it before the Lord as he pleaded for God's help and direction (37:14–20). The Lord answered the faithful king's fervent prayer through Isaiah, assuring him that the Assyrians would not come into the city or even shoot an arrow there (37:21–35).

That night the promised blast, or plague, befell the besieging Assyrian army as the angel of the Lord went through the camp, slaying the attackers (37:36). Giving up the campaign, Sennacherib returned as promised to his own land, where he was assassinated by two of his own sons (37:37–38). As Isaiah prophesied, the king of Assyria heard a rumor, suffered a "blast," returned to his home, and died there by the sword. Though the Assyrians had invaded Judah like a flood, conquering many cities, reaching even up to the neck, Jerusalem, the head and capital, did not fall (8:7–8). Though the Assyrians had reached the spiritual center of the promised land, they enjoyed no victory but rather were broken and trodden under foot upon God's mountain (14:24–25). Though their forces appeared an unconquerable foe, they were chased and dispersed like chaff in the wind (17:12–14).

LIKENING ISAIAH'S WORDS UNTO OURSELVES

We can learn much about how to pray effectively from Hezekiah's example as he went to the house of the Lord to plead for help and direction. He began his fervent petition by bearing his testimony, recognizing the place and power of God (37:16). When we likewise confess our testimonies and gratitude in prayer, we strengthen our faith, thereby increasing our ability to access the powers of heaven.

Hezekiah next carefully explained the crises he and his people were facing (37:17–19). Certainly Hezekiah understood that God was already aware of the problem. Surely he knew that God had a better understanding of the issue than any mortal ever could. The king was describing the problem not for God's benefit but for his own. Hezekiah apparently understood that when we take time in prayer to discuss and describe our challenges we prepare ourselves to receive answers. As we strive to verbalize our concerns and needs to God, we increase our ability to see our situations from God's perspective. We invite the Spirit to place feelings in our hearts and thoughts in our minds that help us identify solutions and proper courses of action. We begin to understand God's will and bring our own in harmony with it. We receive revelation. Hezekiah was then able to confidently ask the Lord to save his people from the Assyrians, expressing his understanding to God that in doing so, "all the kingdoms of the earth may know that thou art the Lord, even thou only" (37:20).

As we follow Hezekiah's example in our own prayers, taking time to express our faith and gratitude to God, as well as carefully discussing our challenges and needs with Him, we find our prayers can be better directed by the Spirit. We come to better know, understand, and accept the will of God. We find our own will conforming to His. We make progress in becoming like Him.

QUESTIONS TO PONDER

1. How is Hezekiah's response as recorded in 37:1–2 a model for us in times of adversity?

2. What can we learn from the reference to the people in 37:22 as the "virgin daughter of Zion?" (compare 3:16–26).

Chapter 35

"I SHALL GO SOFTLY ALL MY YEARS"

ISAIAH 38

A remarkable event in Hezekiah's life that occurred before the Assyrian invasion of Judah in 701 B.C. is chronicled in Isaiah 38. The flashback recounts an event that bears witness to God's omniscience and mercy. Hezekiah had become seriously ill, and Isaiah informed him that he would not recover, for he was appointed to die (38:1). Hezekiah fervently petitioned the Lord that he might live and was subsequently granted fifteen additional years of life (38:2–8, 21–22). The grateful king expressed his thanks through a beautiful psalm of praise (38:9–20).

LIKENING ISAIAH'S WORDS UNTO OURSELVES

In his marvelous work *Faith Precedes the Miracle* (pages 103–4), President Spencer W. Kimball taught: "Everyone must die. Death is an important part of life. Of course, we are never quite ready for the change. Not knowing when it should come, we properly fight to retain our life. Yet we ought not be afraid of death. We pray for the sick, we administer to the afflicted, we implore the Lord to heal and reduce pain and save life and postpone death, and properly so, but not because eternity is so frightful." President Kimball further explained that "many people die before 'their time' because they are careless, abuse their bodies, take unnecessary chances, or expose themselves to hazards, accidents, and sickness." He continued, "I believe we may die prematurely but seldom exceed our time very much. One exception was Hezekiah, 25-year-old king of Judah who was far more godly than his successors or predecessors."

Adding fifteen years to Hezekiah's life proved to be a blessing not only for the king but also for all of Judah. Hezekiah used the extra years well. During those years he strengthened the people's devotion to Jehovah, eliminated apostate practices at high places by centralizing temple worship in Jerusalem, and fortified Jerusalem by repairing breaches in the walls and digging a tunnel to provide water in the event of a siege of the capital (22:9–11; 36:7; 2 Kings 18:1–7). All this he did to prepare his people for the Assyrian attack he knew would come.

When the Assyrians arrived at Jerusalem, they found the faith of the people unshakable. Through their trust and devotion to God the besieged people were able to gain His help. He heard their cries and sent an angel to smite the camp of the Assyrians (37:36). God's promise to Hezekiah when He extended his days was realized (38:6). A great deliverance was granted, and a miraculous victory obtained.

Though we may not enjoy the luxury of knowing exactly when the days of our mortal sojourn will come to an end, we can and should follow Hezekiah's example of using our years, even each day, to strengthen our faith and prepare our defenses against the adversary. We should put away those influences that would weaken our testimonies, build defenses to protect ourselves, especially in areas where we are weakest, and strive to do the will of God. By so doing we too can find our faith fortified and sufficient to withstand the onslaught of those who would seek our captivity and misery. We too will be able to confidently call upon the Lord in our times of challenge and distress.

QUESTIONS TO PONDER

1. What can Isaiah 38 teach about the fragile and precious nature of human existence to those who are approaching death themselves or are mourning the loss of a loved one?

2. What is the conclusion of Hezekiah's psalm recorded in 38:9–20?

Chapter 36

"HEAR THE WORD OF THE LORD"

ISAIAI₹ 39

I saiah 39 records that upon learning of Hezekiah's miraculous recovery, the king of Babylon sent emissaries to Jerusalem with letters and gifts of congratulations to the ruler of Judah (39:1). The act appeared to be a kind political gesture on Babylon's part, and the emissaries were well received in Jerusalem. At the time Babylon was not yet the empire-building world threat that it would become when the Assyrians were conquered, and so Hezekiah apparently had no reservations about giving his Babylonian guests a royal tour of his capital. He showed them his treasures, houses, and fortifications. Indeed, "there was nothing in house, nor in all his dominion, that Hezekiah shewed them not" (39:2).

After the Babylonian delegation departed, Isaiah approached Hezekiah with three questions, "What said these men?" "From whence came they unto thee?" and "What have they seen?" (39:3–4). Hezekiah enthusiastically replied that they came from Babylon and "all that is in my house have they seen" (39:3–4). The king's enthusiasm likely waned when Isaiah told him that

113

the day would come when all that was in Hezekiah's house, including his children, would be carried away into Babylon.

LIKENING ISAIAH'S WORDS UNTO OURSELVES

Obviously, Hezekiah had erred in showing the Babylonians the treasures of his house. We can imagine that the emissaries returned to Babylon with glowing reports of all they had been shown in Jerusalem. Once Babylon began building its empire, tales of the riches of Jerusalem would have made the conquest of Judah an important objective.

Had Hezekiah inquired of the Lord or His prophet, he likely would have been warned against showing the treasures of the kingdom to future power mongers. Alma advised, "Counsel with the Lord in all thy doings, and he will direct thee for good" (Alma 37:37). Hezekiah surely learned the wisdom of that advice through this experience. He was a remarkable man, close to the Lord, faithful and true, but even such a good man can err should he fail to seek counsel from the Lord when making important decisions. How fortunate we are to have a loving Heavenly Father who is anxious to counsel us, always available and always right. If we develop a habit of consulting with the Lord, we can be led to make correct decisions throughout our lives.

QUESTIONS TO PONDER

1. For what decisions in life do we seek divine instruction?

2. What can we learn from Hezekiah's response to Isaiah's prophecy? (39:5–8).

Chapter 37

"HE SHALL FEED HIS FLOCK"

ISAIAɦ 40

Isaiah 40 introduces the prophecies of redemption and restoration that constitute the closing section of Isaiah's prophecies (40–66). It presents the credentials of Jehovah as one who is willing and able to save, restore, and bless His people (40:1–17, 21–31), in contrast to idols and graven images that can do nothing (40:18–20).

LIKENING ISAIAH'S WORDS UNTO OURSELVES

In *Lectures on Faith* we learn that for "any rational and intelligent being" to "exercise faith in God unto life and salvation," he or she must have "a correct idea of [God's] character, perfections, and attributes" (lecture 3, paragraphs 2, 4). As we study Isaiah 40 we find couched in inspiring poetry a wonderful description and testimony of the Lord that can help us better learn and teach of His "character, perfections, and attributes" and affirm our faith in the process. Here Isaiah teaches us that God is omnipotent, or all-powerful (40:3–5, 12, 15–17, 22–25), that He is omniscient, or all-knowing (40:13–14, 26, 28), that He is omnipresent, meaning that His power and influence are both

115

everywhere and eternal (40:6–8, 21, 28), and that He is omni-benevolent, or all-loving and good (40:1–2, 9–11, 29).

Reason indeed tells us that for us to have "faith in God unto life and salvation," we must share Isaiah's testimony of the nature and attributes of God. For example, if we do not believe God is omnipotent, we might reason that we cannot place our faith in Him, for He might not have power to save us. If we do not believe God is omniscient, we might reason that we cannot place our faith in Him, for He might not be intelligent enough to save us. If we do not believe God is omnipresent, we might reason that we cannot place our faith in Him, for He might not be available at our time of need or in the right place to save us. If we do not believe God is omnibenevolent, we might reason that we cannot place our faith in God, for He might not love us enough to save us. But Isaiah assures us that we can confidently place our faith in the Lord for He truly is omnipotent, omniscient, omnipresent, and omnibenevolent. He has all the "character, perfections, and attributes" to bring to pass our immortality and eternal life.

QUESTIONS TO PONDER

1. If God possesses all power, intelligence, goodness, and presence, does He still have a work to do? What is that work?

2. How does waiting on the Lord renew our strength? (40:31).

Chapter 38

"I HAVE CHOSEN THEE"

ISAIAH 41

Isaiah 41 compares the power of the Lord to that of impotent idols. The Lord illustrates His agency and omniscience by declaring that it is He who raised up the righteous man from the east (41:1–5) and the one from the north who will call upon His name (41:25–27). This conquering deliverer is a type for the Messiah, often identified with Abraham or the magnanimous Persian king Cyrus, who allowed the Jews to return from Babylon. Moreover, the Lord chose Israel to be his servant (41:8–9) and will strengthen, protect, and help His chosen people (41:14). He will make them mighty in battle, enabling them to thresh and winnow their enemies (41:15–16). He will nurture and care for the poor and needy among them (41:17). He will give them water and make their land to flourish (41:18–20). He will do all this so that Israel "may see, and know, and consider, and understand" what "the hand of the Lord hath done" (41:20).

In contrast, idols have no volition but must be manufactured by carpenters and goldsmiths (41:6–7). They cannot act or reveal the future and are but vanity, confusion, and an abomination to those who choose them (41:21–24, 29).

LIKENING ISAIAH'S WORDS UNTO OURSELVES

Isaiah makes the point well that, unlike inanimate idols, the Lord is active in the lives of His people. He has power and agency to bless, guide, protect, and nurture His chosen people. Some struggle to reconcile the concept that God has a chosen people and yet is "no respecter of persons" (Acts 10:34). How can He favor a chosen people if He loves all?

Two principles can help resolve the paradox. First, we must remember that being chosen means one has a calling. It makes one more responsible, "for of him unto whom much is given much is required; and he who sins against the greater light shall receive the greater condemnation" (D&C 82:3). A chosen people has the responsibility to lift, bless, edify, and serve others, following the example of the One chosen to be the Lamb of God. Second, God's selection of a chosen people is not a capricious act. Rather, He chooses those who choose Him. In other words, each of us chooses whether we are to be chosen. Ultimately, God wishes all of His children would choose to be chosen. "He inviteth them all to come unto him and partake of his goodness" (2 Nephi 26:33). Isaiah assures us if we choose to be chosen, "the Lord thy God will hold thy right hand, saying unto thee, Fear not, I will help thee" (41:13).

QUESTIONS TO PONDER

1. What characteristics of spiritual servitude does 41:8–9 present?

2. What could be the significance of the right hand in 41:10, 13?

Chapter 39

"BEHOLD MY SERVANT"

ISAIAH 42

The later chapters of Isaiah contain a series of beautiful poetic prophecies about a servant who will bless the world through his life, labors, and suffering. Collectively these prophecies are known as the Servant Songs or the Servant Psalms. The Servant Songs typically include Isaiah 42:1–7; 49:1–7; 50:4–9; 52:13–15; and 53:1–12.

The identity of the servant has been much debated. Some speculate that the servant is Isaiah himself. Others suggest that perhaps the servant is Cyrus, the great king who allowed the captive Jews to return to Judah. Still others view the servant as the house of Israel as a whole. Indeed a case can be made for each of these individuals or entities, and others, to be a fulfillment of some of the Servant Song prophecies. Latter-day Saints typically identify the Servant as Jesus Christ, for He fulfills *all* the prophecies of the Servant Songs, and there are some only He can fulfill. Thus, although other individuals or entities, such as Isaiah, Cyrus, or the house of Israel, fulfill portions of the prophecies in the Servant Songs, they are best viewed as a type or a symbol for Jesus Christ, the Servant who fulfills them all.

119

The Servant Song that opens Isaiah 42 is given in the context of demonstrating the omniscience and omnipotence of God. In the song we learn about the promised Servant's election, relationship with God, and ministry (42:1–7; 19–20; see also JST 42:19–20). After describing the wonderful things the Servant will do, the Lord testifies in stirring poetic language of His power, agency, and benevolence (42:8–16, 21, 23–25) and again chastises those who put their trust in idols rather than in Him (42:17–18; 22–23).

LIKENING ISAIAH'S WORDS UNTO OURSELVES

In our day we recognize how Jesus Christ fulfilled what was promised in the Servant Song in Isaiah 42. For example, as prophesied in the opening verse, we understand that the relationship between the Father and the Son is one of unity, love, trust, and support. We know that Christ did indeed serve the Father and that the Father upheld and supported the Son. We understand that God elected, or chose, the Son for the work and delighted in Him. We can see in Christ's ministry how the Spirit of God truly was upon Him as He served. We know that His ministry blessed not only Israel but also the Gentiles (42:1, 6).

We further understand how Christ's mortal ministry conformed to the description given in Isaiah 42. His ministry was relatively quiet and gentle: He did "not cry, nor lift up, nor cause his voice to be heard in the street," and His actions were so tender and quiet that even a delicate, bruised or damaged reed was not broken thereby, nor was a feeble "smoking flax" or smoldering wick of a lamp quenched by His passing (42:2–3). Christ's mortal coming was largely unnoticed by most of contemporary humankind. He was born to a humble woman in simple surroundings and raised in modest and quiet circumstances in an obscure village in a relatively unremarkable part of the ancient world. During His life His teachings were mostly unknown beyond His own people and land, and His death drew little notice in the Roman Empire.

Likewise, we know that though His mortal ministry was relatively quiet and unnoticed, He did indeed establish truth and justice on the earth and fulfilled His mission (42:3–4). We can confidently testify that He is our Creator and the Giver of life in fulfillment of God's plan and covenant (42:5–6). We know that He brought light to the Gentiles, opened the eyes of the blind, and set prisoners free (42:6–7).

QUESTIONS TO PONDER

1. What parts of the prophecy found in 42:1–7 have been fulfilled? What is now being fulfilled? What is yet to be fulfilled?

2. Who are the prisoners and what are the prisons from which the Servant brings freedom? (42:7).

3. What does the clarification of 42:19–20 that is found in the Joseph Smith Translation mean for us?

Chapter 40

"BESIDE ME THERE IS NO SAVIOUR"

ISAIAH 43

𝕿he testimony of the power, agency, wisdom, and love of God continues in Isaiah 43. The Lord assures us that He is our Redeemer, Savior, Creator, Guide, Protector, Defender, and Healer (43:1–21). Though the people of Israel had failed to worship, obey, and recognize Him (43:21–24, 27–28), they are invited once again to remember Him, plead with Him, and be justified by Him (43:25–26).

LIKENING ISAIAH'S WORDS UNTO OURSELVES

Among the distinguishing doctrines of Latter-day Saints is the understanding that God the Father and God the Son are separate, distinct beings who share a common purpose, work, and glory. Latter-day Saints further understand that the Lord, Jehovah, the God who spoke to Abraham, Isaac, and Jacob, who parted the Red Sea and fed Israel manna in the wilderness is the same being who became known as Jesus of Nazareth in mortality. Divinely invested with the authority of the Father, Jesus Christ is the God of the Old Testament.

One way we come to this doctrinal understanding of Jesus

Christ is through Isaiah 43. The Lord explains, "I am the LORD thy God, the Holy One of Israel, thy Saviour" (43:3) and later repeats "I, even I, am the LORD; and beside me there is no saviour" (43:11). In the King James Version of the Old Testament, the word LORD is written in one large and three small capital letters when it is used to translate the four letters of the Hebrew term that scholars call the Tetragrammaton, a Greek word meaning "four letters." Transliterated, the four letters would be *YHWH.* Those four letters are often used in the Old Testament for the name of God—Yahweh. It is a sacred name, especially to our Jewish brothers and sisters. Accordingly, when they read the text they do not try to pronounce the sacred name Yahweh. Instead, they may say "*hashem,*" which means "the name," or "*adonai,*" which means "lord." Out of respect for that practice, the King James translators rendered the meaning of the four letters of the Tetragrammaton as "LORD," in one large and three small capital letters, to indicate that the Hebrew word is actually "YHWH" rather than "*adonai.*"

Whenever the Tetragrammaton appears in the standard Hebrew text, the Masoretic text of the Old Testament, the vowels of the word *adonai* are written underneath the four consonants *YHWH,* apparently to remind the reader to say *adonai* rather than the sacred name. If we were to read the Tetragrammaton aloud using the vowels from the word *adonai,* it would sound something like "Yehowah," which in English we would pronounce "Jehovah." This practice contributed to *Jehovah* becoming the name that we give to the God of the Old Testament. Accordingly, wherever "LORD" appears in the Old Testament, we can substitute the name Jehovah.

Thus we can read from this chapter, "For I am [Jehovah] thy God, the Holy One of Israel, thy Savior" and "I, even I, am

[Jehovah]; and beside me there is no saviour" (43:3, 11). The language is clear. Jehovah is the only Savior. The reasoning is simple. If the Lord Jehovah is our only Savior, and Jesus Christ is our only Savior, then the Lord Jehovah must be Jesus Christ.

Somehow, even before He obtained a mortal body, Jesus had become so like the Father that He was divinely invested with the power and authority to be Jehovah, the God of the Old Testament, who loved us enough to condescend from that position of power and authority to take upon Himself mortality and work the great and infinite Atonement.

QUESTIONS TO PONDER

1. How can Doctrine and Covenants 132:19–20 inform our interpretation of the last phrase in 43:10?

2. What can we learn from the water imagery in 42:2, 16, 19?

Chapter 41

"HE FEEDETH ON ASHES"

ISAIAH 44

Like a refrain to the message of Isaiah 41, Isaiah 44 echoes the contrast between the power, agency, and benevolence of Jehovah and the absolute nothingness of idols. Here with stirring poetry the Lord reminds us that He chooses, He creates, He blesses, He reveals, He redeems, He delivers, He restores, He protects, He atones—He exists (44:1–8, 21–28). In contrast, idols cannot create but must be created. They cannot give strength to idolaters but drain it from them. They cannot provide but must be provided for. They cannot move but must be moved. They cannot act but only be acted upon (44:9–20). There is considerable sarcasm and irony as the Lord describes how foolish men cut down a tree, use part of it for heating, and use part of it for cooking and with the residue he makes a god (44:14–17). He wonders why none can see the silliness of worshiping the stock of a tree (44:18–19).

LIKENING ISAIAH'S WORDS UNTO OURSELVES

We recognize that idolatry was not a problem unique to Isaiah's time or people. In our day, too, anything we make more

important in our lives than God, any act or thing to which
we are willing to give greater time, resources, homage, or devotion than our Heavenly Father becomes our idol. They feed
"on ashes," the Lord declares of such idolaters, and they have a
"deceived heart" incapable of seeing the "lie" they hold in their
"right hand" (44:20). The imagery is profound. We can picture
a man with a gnawing hunger in his belly, ravenously scooping
up handfuls of ashes with his right hand to stuff into his mouth.
Chewing and swallowing, he may actually be able to consume
enough to satisfy his appetite for a time. He may even reach a
point where he declares, "I'm so full I couldn't eat another ash,"
but in his misguided attempts to satisfy his cravings he fails to
provide for himself that which he truly needs. There is no nour-
ishment in ashes. Indeed, one can have a belly full of ashes and
still die of malnutrition.

We would certainly be guilty of believing a lie if we thought
eating ashes could sustain life. Even so, we certainly believe a lie
if we seek real happiness, fulfillment, and joy in things, idols, or
acts contrary to the will of God. Though we may successfully
assuage our hunger for a time with such acts or things, there is
no lasting substance, nothing of eternal value, in them. They
are ashes that deceive us. How much better if "we press forward with a steadfastness in Christ, having a perfect brightness
of hope, and a love of God and of all men, . . . feasting upon
the word of Christ, and endure to the end," for then the Father
assures, "Ye shall have eternal life" (2 Nephi 31:20).

QUESTIONS TO PONDER

1. How do we distinguish between ashes and nourishing sustenance? (44:20).

2. In what situations may we find help and direction in the
   teachings of Isaiah 44?

Chapter 42

"I AM THE LORD,
AND THERE IS NONE ELSE"

ISAIAH 45

In the final verse of Isaiah 44, as the Lord lists some of the wonderful things He has done and will yet do for His people, He identifies Cyrus, the mighty Persian who conquered Babylon (ca. 538 B.C.), as the one He will raise up to rebuild Jerusalem and the temple (44:28). This prophecy introduces Isaiah 45, which records a message directed to Cyrus.

Cyrus was a type for Christ as he conquered Babylon, restored the covenant people to their promised land, and helped them rebuild their cities, lives, and faith (compare 41:2, 25). In this prophecy, given about two centuries before Cyrus's birth, the Lord calls Cyrus by name, referring to him as His anointed, one raised up and empowered by God to conquer nations for the sake of Israel (45:1–4). The Lord describes His power and works for Cyrus (45:5–8, 11–12) and admonishes the king to recognize His role in his establishment (9–10). After describing what God has done for him, the Lord tells Cyrus what he must do in return. Cyrus is to rebuild Jerusalem and let His "captive" people go (45:13). After the instructions to Cyrus, Isaiah 45 continues testifying of God's power and efforts to redeem and restore His people (45:14–25).

LIKENING ISAIAH'S WORDS UNTO OURSELVES

The remarkable prophecy to Cyrus poignantly demonstrates the omniscience of God. We may wonder why God would speak to Cyrus, calling him by name centuries before the king was born. The Jewish historian Josephus helps answer that question:

"In the first year of the reign of Cyrus, which was the seventieth from the day that our people were removed out of their own land into Babylon, God commiserated the captivity and calamity of these poor people, according as he had foretold to them by Jeremiah the prophet, before the destruction of the city, that after they had served Nebuchadnezzar and his posterity, and after they had undergone that servitude seventy years, he would restore them again to the land of their fathers, and they should build their temple, and enjoy their ancient prosperity; and these things God did afford them; for he stirred up the mind of Cyrus, and made him write this throughout all Asia:—'Thus saith Cyrus the king:—Since God Almighty hath appointed me to be king of the habitable earth, I believe that he is that God which the nation of the Israelites worship; for indeed he foretold my name by the prophets, and that I should build him a house at Jerusalem, in the country of Judea.'

"This was known to Cyrus by his reading the book which Isaiah left behind him of his prophecies; for this prophet said that God had spoken thus to him in a secret vision:—'My will is, that Cyrus, whom I have appointed to be king over many and great nations, send back my people to their own land, and build my temple.' This was foretold by Isaiah one hundred and forty years before the temple was demolished. Accordingly, when

Cyrus read this, and admired the divine power, an earnest desire and ambition seized upon him to fulfil what was so written; so he called for the most eminent Jews that were in Babylon, and said to them, that he gave them leave to go back to their own country, and to rebuild their city Jerusalem, and the temple of God, for that he would be their assistant, and that he would write to the rulers and governors that were in the neighborhood of their country of Judea, that they should contribute to them gold and silver for the building of the temple, and, besides that, beasts for their sacrifices" (Josephus, *Antiquities of the Jews,* 11:1–2).

Just as the Lord planned far ahead to provide for the restoration of His people through Cyrus, we can have confidence that He has planned far ahead, even before the foundation of the world, to redeem, restore, and save us. In order to lay claim to the blessings, like Cyrus we need to do our part, trusting and obeying His will, remembering the assurance He gives, "I am the Lord, and there is none else" (45:5, 6, 18; see also vv. 14, 21).

QUESTIONS TO PONDER

1. If the Lord spoke to you as He did Cyrus, what would He say about the blessings He has given you and what He expects of you in return?

2. In addition to the commission to free His people and rebuild His city (45:13), what else did God want Cyrus and us to understand? (see 45:3, 5, 6, 7, 18, 19, 22).

Chapter 43

"THEY ARE A BURDEN"

ISAIAH 46

Repeating a theme of Isaiah 41 and 44, Isaiah 46 again illustrates the foolishness of idolatry by contrasting the Lord's power to the helplessness of idols (compare 41; 44). Here the Lord notes that the Babylonian gods Bel and Nebo are nothing more than useless, inanimate objects—a burden to the men who fashion them and the beasts forced to transport them (46:1–2, 5–8). In contrast, the Lord makes, carries, bears, and delivers His people (46:3–4). He is the only true God (46:9), who reveals truth (46:9–10), who raises up deliverers (46:11), who has power to accomplish all His will (46:10–11), and who will save and glorify Israel (46:12–13).

LIKENING ISAIAH'S WORDS UNTO OURSELVES

The image of men struggling to lug around great, useless burdens of their own creation is both comical and profound. It causes each of us to consider, "Is there a Nebo or a Bel in my life—things or activities of little or no real value or eternal consequence with which I have burdened myself?" or "Am I giving too much of my time or means to labors, entities or

objects that cannot bless, save or redeem?" How much better
to give our heart, soul, and might (Deuteronomy 6:5) to the
work and worship of the One who can carry us, forgive us, remove our burdens, show us the way, and save us. Christ extends
His invitation to all: "Come unto me, all ye that labour and are
heavy laden, and I will give you rest. Take my yoke upon you,
and learn of me; for I am meek and lowly in heart: and ye shall
find rest unto your souls. For my yoke is easy, and my burden is
light" (Matthew 11:28–30).

QUESTIONS TO PONDER

1. What or who are the Bels and the Nebos that burden us?
   (46:1–2).

2. How do we invite or allow the Lord to carry us? How?

Chapter 44

"THE WIDOW BABYLON"

ISAIAH 47

With vivid imagery the prophet foretells in Isaiah 47 how proud and pampered Babylon will become like a humiliated slave and be left forsaken and barren (47:1–5, 7–9). Her punishment will be just recompense for her mercilessness, haughtiness, and conceit (47:6, 7–10). All this will befall her despite her acclaimed astrologers, sorcerers, and prognosticators (47:11–13). These diviners will not be able to save Babylon—or themselves (47:14–15).

LIKENING ISAIAH'S WORDS UNTO OURSELVES

This prophecy of the destruction of Babylon drips with irony. Babylon was a center of worldly wealth, pride, prestige, arrogance, and corruption. That she should become a humble slave, forced to do menial tasks for her master (47:2), destitute with no hope of husband or progeny (47:7–9) must have sounded unbelievable to Isaiah's contemporaries—yet ancient Babylon was reduced to rubble many centuries ago and its proud and wealthy inhabitants conquered, dispersed and forgotten.

Babylon was also a center of science and sorcery. The people prided themselves on their ability to foresee the future and ward off evil. Through their astrologers, prognosticators, and heptascopers (those who try to see into the future by examining the entrails of slaughtered animals), they felt confident they would not be caught unawares. Yet Babylon fell quickly and unexpectedly on October 11, 538 B.C., when Cyrus, king of the Persians, diverted the Euphrates River that coursed under the city walls and sent his soldiers into the heart of the city along the empty riverbed, surprising the Babylonians as they reveled at a festival.

The prophecy and its fulfillment anciently remind us today that those who glory in their own worldly wealth, wisdom, prestige, or power are placing their future and happiness on fragile and fleeting footing. Only by loving God first and most, following His great plan of happiness, can we lay claim to real and lasting joy. Babylon will fall.

QUESTIONS TO PONDER

1. How do we avoid developing the Babylonian attitude described in 47:7, 10?

2. What are some modern equivalents of the stargazers, prognosticators, and sorcerers described in 47:12–13?

Chapter 45

"THEN HAD THY PEACE BEEN AS A RIVER"

ISAIAH 48

Isaiah 48 and 49 are the first of Isaiah's writings to appear in the Book of Mormon (1 Nephi 20). Nephi quoted the chapters to his brethren that he "might more fully persuade them to believe in the Lord their Redeemer" (1 Nephi 19:23). Before quoting the chapters, he encouraged all who are a "remnant of the house of Israel" to "liken them [the words of Isaiah] unto yourselves, that ye may have hope" (1 Nephi 19:24).

Isaiah 48 begins with a divine dialogue that demonstrates God's patience, determination, and mercy. The Lord speaks to those who "are come forth out of the waters of Judah" (48:1), or the waters of baptism (1 Nephi 20:1), who act as if they are righteous and obedient but in truth are not (48:1–2). Though they are stubborn and obstinate, with brows like brass and necks like iron, the Lord will yet declare that which is to come even to this hypocritical portion of the covenant people, lest they ascribe God's work to their idols or to their own genius (48:3–8). Moreover, the Lord assures these rebellious people that He will not cut them off immediately, reminding them that they were refined and chosen in the furnace of affliction (48:9–11).

Rather, He invites them to hearken and come unto Him, their Creator and Redeemer (48:12–19). He encourages them to flee Babylon, promising them that if they do, He will provide for them, even as He provided waters to flow out of the rock for their forefathers in the wilderness (48:20–22).

LIKENING ISAIAH'S WORDS UNTO OURSELVES

As the Lord pleads with Israel to follow Him, He testifies, "O that thou hadst hearkened to my commandments! then had thy peace been as a river, and thy righteousness as the waves of the sea; thy seed also had been as the sand, and the offspring of thy bowels like the gravel thereof" (48:18–19). The imagery of flowing water and innumerable progeny point to a doctrine fundamental to our faith—the doctrine that we can become like our Father in Heaven.

The Lord used imagery of flowing water to describe the blessings of accepting and following Him as He spoke to the Samaritan woman at the well during His mortal ministry. He invited her to partake of the living water that He, who is its wellspring, offered. He promised, "Whosoever drinketh of the water that I shall give him shall never thirst; but the water that I shall give him shall be in him a well of water springing up into everlasting life" (John 4:14). Latter-day Saints see profound doctrine in this promise, for it assures us that if we are willing to partake of Christ and His gospel, then not only will we find our spiritual thirst eternally satiated but we too can become a source of living water. We too can be a well springing up into eternal life. In a very real sense we can become like Christ, our Fount.

In a revelation given to Joseph Smith while he was imprisoned in Liberty Jail, the Lord again used the imagery of flowing water to teach the same truth. There He taught the Prophet

about the power of the priesthood and the conditions upon
which its power could be accessed (D&C 121:34–44). God revealed the blessings in store for those who faithfully use priesthood power, who have charity towards all men, and who let
virtue garnish their thoughts unceasingly. To such he promised,
"Then shall thy confidence wax strong in the presence of God;
and the doctrine of the priesthood shall distil upon thy soul as
the dews from heaven. The Holy Ghost shall be thy constant
companion, and thy scepter an unchanging scepter of righteousness and truth; and thy dominion shall be an everlasting
dominion, and without compulsory means it shall *flow* unto
thee forever and ever" (D&C 121:45–46; emphasis added).
Latter-day Saints see in this kingship imagery of an unchanging
scepter of righteousness and an eternally flowing dominion not
only a description of God as our King but also, again, a promise
that we can become like Him. Through righteousness we too
can enjoy an everlasting and flowing dominion as rulers, even
kings holding sure scepters of righteousness and truth.

This promise given to the Samaritan woman at the well and
to the Prophet Joseph Smith in the Liberty Jail echoes that given
by the Lord in Isaiah 48: If we are obedient to the will of the
Lord, we can become like Him, for our peace will be as a river
and our righteousness as the waves of the sea (48:18). To clarify
that He is promising exaltation, the Lord explained, "Thy seed
also had been as the sand, and the offspring of thy bowels like
the gravel thereof" (48:19). The blessing of innumerable posterity for those who realize the promise of righteousness reminds
us of the assurance given in another revelation to Joseph Smith
in which we are told that those who become like God will have
"a continuation of the seeds forever and ever. Then shall they
be gods, because they have no end; therefore shall they be from

everlasting to everlasting" (D&C 132:19–20). Thus the Lord taught in Isaiah's day, in New Testament times, and in our dispensation the great truth that man, created in the image of God, has the potential to become like Him, enjoying an ever-flowing dominion of righteousness and eternal increase.

QUESTIONS TO PONDER

1. What specifically is required in our dispensation to enjoy peace as a river and seed innumerable as the sand? (48:18–19).

2. How do we go forth from Babylon with a voice of singing today? (48:29).

Chapter 46

"THESE, WHERE HAD THEY BEEN?"

ISAIAH 49

Isaiah 49 opens with another Servant Song (compare Isaiah 42). As Nephi quoted Isaiah 49 to his brothers, he included a significant introduction that helps us identify the isles to whom this prophecy is addressed. While our current Old Testament version begins with simple imperative, "Listen, O isles, unto me" (49:1), Nephi's version begins, "And again: Hearken, O ye house of Israel, all ye that are broken off and are driven out because of the wickedness of the pastors of my people; yea, all ye that are broken off, that are scattered abroad, who are of my people, O house of Israel. Listen, O isles, unto me" (1 Nephi 21:1). Thus we learn that *isles,* as used in Isaiah, refers to the scattered covenant people.

After this introduction the Servant speaks to the isles in the first person. His words add a second witness to many of the truths taught in the first Servant Song (42:1–7). We are taught again that the Servant was chosen and called early, even "from the womb" (49:1, 5; see also 42:1). We are taught again that the Servant will be a "light to the Gentiles" (49:6; see also 42:1, 6), that he would be supported by the Father (49:8; see also 42:1, 6), and that he

138

would free, feed, guide, and gather the prisoners from the ends of the earth (49:9–13; see also 42:7).

The Servant further explains that though he is both well prepared and powerful, having his mouth made "like a sharp sword" and being a "polished shaft," yet he is hidden in the Father's hand and kept in the Father's quiver (49:2), reminding us again that the mortal Messiah conducted His ministry humbly and quietly, in a part of the world that many of His contemporaries would have considered obscure and unimportant (see also 42:2–3).

The paradox continues in the following verses as the Servant presents opposing perspectives on the accomplishments of His mortal ministry. He observes that while on one hand His strength and labor might appear to have been spent in vain, for "Israel be not gathered," yet on the other hand He will have accomplished God's work and is to be judged of the Lord (49:5). In response to the Servant's observation, God assures Him that though Jacob may not be gathered during His mortal ministry, His efforts would still be pleasing and glorious to the Lord, and God will strengthen Him (49:5). Thus we understand that while to some it might appear that Christ spent His labor and strength in vain, the Father knows that His Servant's work will bring salvation unto the end of the earth (49:4, 6). Though He may be despised of men, ultimately He is chosen of God, and kings and princes will come to worship Him (49:7).

After the Servant Song, the Lord assures the isles that though they may feel forsaken, He has not—and, in fact, cannot—forget them, for they are graven upon the palms of His hands (49:14–16). With further stirring imagery, the Lord then reveals how He will gather and restore His scattered and lost people (49:18–26).

LIKENING ISAIAH'S WORDS UNTO OURSELVES

As the Lord explains how He is working to gather and re-store His people, He foretells a time when those who thought the Lord had forsaken them (49:14) will lift up their eyes and be surprised to find a vast gathering of covenant children whom they knew nothing about—so many that they will struggle to find room for them all and be led to exclaim, "Who hath begotten me these . . . these, where had they been?" (49:21). Apparently they will be surprised to learn that rather than for-saking His children as they had supposed, the Lord was actually doing a great work among a people they did not recognize as part of the covenant family. The Lord identifies these lost chil-dren who will finally be numbered among the house of Israel as he declares, "I will lift up mine hand to the Gentiles, and set up my standard to the people: and they shall bring thy sons in their arms, and thy daughters shall be carried upon their shoulders" (49:22; compare 54:1–3).

This remarkable prophecy raises the question, "Who are these Gentiles who will help gather scattered Israel and eventu-ally be recognized as part of the covenant family?" Latter-day Saints recognize that we ourselves are an answer to that question and a fulfillment of this wonderful prophecy. We are the Gentiles among whom the Lord has set up His standard, or ensign, even the restored gospel of Jesus Christ (compare 11:11–16). The Hebrew term *nes* translated as "standard" in 49:22 is translated as "ensign" in 11:12. The term is used by Isaiah to refer to the flag or standard of the restored gospel to which the covenant people will gather.

Though we sometimes may be "identified with the Gentiles" (D&C 109:60), we anticipate the day when we will be recog-nized by all as part of the covenant family and numbered among the house of Israel (compare 2 Nephi 10:18; 3 Nephi 21:6; 30:2). As stewards of the restored gospel, we further understand our divine mandate to seek out lost sons and daughters and carry them back to the covenant, even to be "nursing fathers" and "nursing mothers" as we assist in the Lord's great work to gather, restore, and redeem His children (49:22–23).

In this prophecy, the Lord likens our gathering to the gospel and our eventual recognition as part of the house of Israel to a bride putting on her wedding apparel: "As I live, saith the Lord, thou shalt surely clothe thee [Israel] with them all [scattered Israel once identified with the Gentiles but now recognized as part of the covenant family], as with an ornament, and bind them on thee, as a bride doeth" (49:18; compare 52:1). A bride puts on her bridal apparel in preparation for the coming of the bridegroom. Christ is the Bridegroom, and the covenant people His bride. Thus the imagery reminds us that as we fulfill our role as the latter-day Gentiles among whom the restored gospel ensign is raised up, we are preparing for the coming of our Bridegroom, the millennial Messiah.

QUESTIONS TO PONDER

1. How can 2:2 enlarge a Latter-day Saint's understanding of 49:11?

2. What principles from 49:13–23 can instruct and inspire modern-day missionaries?

Chapter 47

"YE SHALL LIE DOWN IN SORROW"

ISAIAH 50

I saiah 50 begins with the premise that the Lord and His covenant people have become estranged from each other. The Lord asks a series of questions, inviting Israel to consider how and why they have become so separated from their God (50:1–2). The Lord reminds His children that He still has power—power to deliver them and power to control the elements (50:2–3). Then, to illustrate His love and compassion for them, the Lord again assumes the voice of the Servant, speaking in another Servant Song to describe what He will experience, endure, and accomplish in mortality in behalf of His children (50:4–9).

In the song the Servant acknowledges God's hand in preparing for the work and supporting Him in it, giving Him the tongue of the learned, wakening and opening His ears so that He could learn (50:4–5). The Servant then speaks of the persecution He will endure as He willingly allows Himself to be smitten and spat upon (50:5–6), foreshadowing the cruel treatment He would receive at the hands of Pilate and the Roman soldiers commissioned to scourge and crucify Him (Matthew 26:31).

The Servant closes the song by testifying of His confidence that God will sustain and support Him, whereas His adversaries will wax old and be eaten up (50:7–9), a prophecy fulfilled as the Roman empire and the Jewish leaders who condemned Him have faded in infamy, while the redeeming work of the Servant is praised and persists through eternity.

Isaiah 50 closes with the Lord's warning that those who choose to walk in the light of their own fires rather than in the light of the Lord will lie down in sorrow (50:10–11).

LIKENING ISAIAH'S WORDS UNTO OURSELVES

In questioning His children about why they have become separated from Him, the Lord asks them to present evidence that it was His choice. "Where is the bill of your mother's divorcement, whom I have put away? or which of my creditors is it to whom I have sold you?" To His own questions the Lord answers, "Behold, for your iniquities have ye sold yourselves, and for your transgressions is your mother put away" (50:1). The reasoning reminds us of the profound counsel, "If you find yourself further from God today than you were yesterday, ask yourself, 'Who moved?'"

We can be assured that the sincere answer to such a question will always be the same. God is ever present and willing to guide, bless, and even forgive those who are striving to love and follow Him. He is constant. He does not move away from us but waits with open and anxious arms to embrace those who have used their agency to wander away from Him, should they choose to return and repent. Indeed, He became the Servant to make possible such a reunion and reconciliation.

QUESTIONS TO PONDER

1. How do we sell ourselves? How do we rescue one who has sold himself? (50:1).

2. How do we know if we are walking in the sparks that we have kindled or in the Lord's light? (50:10–11).

Chapter 48

"LOOK UNTO THE ROCK
WHENCE YE ARE HEWN"

ISAIAᕼ 51

Pleading and inviting imperatives spill from Isaiah 51. Those who follow after righteousness are implored to hearken to the Lord and look to their heritage (51:1–3), to hearken and give ear to His law, righteousness, and judgment (51:4–5), to lift up their eyes and look at His salvation (51:6), to hearken to Him and fear not the reproach of temporal man (51:7–8), to awake and stand up as the Lord pours out His cup of fury upon the wicked and raises up sons full of fury to do His work (51:17–20; compare Revelation 11:3–12), and to hear as He takes the cup of trembling, even the dregs of the cup of His fury, and places it in the hand of those who afflict the covenant people (51:21–23).

In the midst of reporting these imperatives to the covenant people Isaiah issues one to the Lord himself, pleading with God to awaken and put on strength to conquer enemies and control the elements as He had in times past, thereby preparing the way for the redeemed to return with joy upon their head, causing sorrow and mourning to flee away (51:9–11). These admonitions

145

all remind us of what our God can do, has done, and will yet do for us if we will but trust and follow Him.

LIKENING ISAIAH'S WORDS UNTO OURSELVES

Most adults can recall a time when, as teenagers heading out for an evening of activities, they were cautioned by their parents, "Remember who you are!" Anxious parents often give such counsel, knowing that if their sons and daughters will keep in mind that they are also children of a loving Heavenly Father with a divine destiny and potential to become like God, they will likely make better choices and avoid decisions that will lead them down wrong paths. It is difficult to sin when remembering who we really are.

As mortal parents encourage their children to remember their divine heritage, they are following the example and practice of our Heavenly Father as He pleads with His children to "look unto the rock whence ye are hewn" and to "look unto Abraham your father, and unto Sarah that bare you" (51:1–2), reminding them of the great promises given by covenant to Abraham and his posterity (51:3), promises of inheritance, protection, posterity, priesthood, and eternal life (compare Genesis 12:1–3; 13:14–17; 15:4–6; 17:1–12; Abraham 2:7–11).

QUESTIONS TO PONDER

1. What does it mean to a Latter-day Saint to be a descendant of Abraham? (51:1–3).

2. How is drinking the dregs of the Lord's cup a voluntary action? (51:17). Is it good or bad for us? What are the alternatives?

Chapter 49

THE SERVANT "MARRED MORE THAN ANY"

ISAIAH 52

In Isaiah 52 the Lord continues to invite and command the covenant people to recognize His power and plans to redeem and bless them. He begins by commanding Zion to "put on thy strength" (52:1), or to "put on the authority of the priesthood, which she, Zion, has a right to by lineage; also to return to that power which she had lost" (D&C 113:7–8), and to "put on thy beautiful garments" (52:1), perhaps again meaning to prepare for the coming of Christ, the millennial Bridegroom (see discussion of Isaiah 49). The Lord assures that as Zion does so, they shall be cleansed, redeemed without money, delivered from oppressors, and come to know their God (52:1–6). Those who declare this gospel, or good tidings, will be blessed and join in the celebration as God once again reigns, Jerusalem is redeemed, and they see eye to eye, even as the Lord bares His holy arm and reveals His salvation (52:7–11; compare Mosiah 12:20–27; 15:10–31). Just as they were delivered from slavery in Egypt anciently, so they are now to depart from their spiritual bondage, touching no unclean thing and having the assurance

147

that their God will both go before them and be their rearguard
(52:11–12).

Isaiah 52 closes with another Servant Song, telling us that
the Servant will be exalted, extolled, and honored even though
"marred more than any man" (52:13–15; see the discussion of
Isaiah 42 for more on Servant Songs).

LIKENING ISAIAH'S WORDS UNTO OURSELVES

The closing Song of Isaiah 52 reveals important truths
about our Savior, the Servant. The passage begins and ends with
praise to the Servant, recognizing His wisdom, His exaltation,
and the reverence He will receive from kings as they learn of
Him (52:13, 15). We see the prophecy fulfilled as we remember
Christ's role as Jehovah in the Old Testament, as we consider
the wisdom manifested in His teachings and actions during His
mortal ministry, as we recognize His place with the Father in the
eternities, and as we learn of kings and rulers who have placed
their faith in Him.

The middle of the Song speaks of the Servant's visage, or
appearance, being marred or disfigured more than that of any
other man (52:14). The language reminds us of Christ's atoning agony that commenced in Gethsemane when He bore the
sins, pains, and sufferings of all humankind throughout all dis-
pensations, bleeding from every pore (Luke 22:39–44; D&C
19:16–19; Alma 7:11–12). Surely in that moment, His visage
was "marred more than any man, and his form more than the
sons of men" (52:14) for no other person born to this earth
could have endured the weight of the atoning suffering.

Perhaps the most poignant doctrine of the passage is revealed in the next phrase, which tells us that He would be so
marred in order to "sprinkle many nations" (52:15). The Joseph

Smith Translation of the Bible substitutes the word "gather" for "sprinkle" in this passage. The substitution makes excellent sense to Latter-day Saints who understand that through His atoning suffering, by being marred more than any, our Savior opened the way for us to be gathered, reunited, and made "at-one" with our Heavenly Father. To the Old Testament people, the original Hebrew word *nazah,* translated as "sprinkle" in the King James Version, likewise would have made excellent sense. This verb occurs often in the Old Testament, typically in the context of purification and sanctification rites. Priests were to "sprinkle" holy water, sacred oil, or sacrificial blood upon individuals, implements, and installations to make them holy, pure, and sanctified (for example, Exodus 29:21; Leviticus 4:6, 17; 14:7, 16, 27, 51; 16:14–15; Numbers 8:7, 17; 19:18–19). Thus those who lived under the Mosaic law would have understood, as do we today, that through His atoning suffering, the Servant, our Savior, would purify and sanctify us.

QUESTIONS TO PONDER

1. How can we sell ourselves for nought and still be redeemed without money? (52:3).

2. How is the prophecy of 52:7 being fulfilled today?

Chapter 50

"THOU SHALT MAKE HIS SOUL AN OFFERING FOR SIN"

ISAIAH 53

I saiah 53 is arguably the most beautiful, sublime, and poignant of the Servant Songs. In this moving prophecy we learn of the Servant's humble beginnings and unassuming appearance (53:1–2). We are told that He will be widely rejected, a "man of sorrows and acquainted with grief" (53:3). We learn of His vicarious sufferings (53:4–6, 8, 10–12) and His willingness to endure oppression, persecution, and injustice (53:7–8). We are told of His incongruous death (53:8) and what His death and suffering can mean for all of humankind (53:9–11).

LIKENING ISAIAH'S WORDS UNTO OURSELVES

Latter-day Saints and other faithful Christians through the ages have been both instructed and inspired by how this accurate and detailed prophecy was fulfilled by our Savior, Jesus of Nazareth. We know that Christ did indeed "grow up before him as a tender plant" (53:2). He did not spring forth suddenly as a mighty oak but rather as a tender plant, born in a tiny and uncelebrated nation to a poor and common couple in the humblest of circumstances. We further understand that He truly was a root out of dry ground (53:2). One would not expect a root to spring forth from dry ground, just as one would not expect a child to be born to a virgin or for a man from a village as obscure as Nazareth to be the Redeemer of the world (compare John 1:45–46).

We know that He looked like an ordinary man. He had "no form nor comeliness," and when men saw Him there was "no beauty that we should desire him" (53:2). Consequently, rather than being recognized, accepted, and esteemed, Christ was "despised and rejected of men" (53:4). Those who followed Him did so for His message rather than His visage. Many turned their backs to hide their faces from Him and viewed Him as one deservedly stricken and smitten of God (53:4). He was indeed oppressed and afflicted, yet He refused to deliver or defend Himself (53:7). He was taken from prison and denied justice, with no apparent friend or posterity to "declare his generation" (53:8). Eventually, he made his grave with the wicked (53:9; compare Luke 23:32–33) and yet was buried with the rich (53:9; compare Matthew 27:57–60). Most important, we know that He took on mortality, lived, suffered, and died for us. He bore "our griefs," carried "our sorrows," and "was wounded for our transgressions"; and "with his stripes we are healed" (53:4–5).

The Hebrew phrase translated in the King James Version as "who shall declare his generation" (53:8) is enigmatic. Some view it as a declaration that the Servant would die without posterity. Others see it as a lament that there would be none to defend Him. The Book of Mormon prophet Abinadi understood the question to be asking who among us are Christ's seed or children (Mosiah 15:10–13). Abinadi's interpretation makes excellent sense, for the answer to the question is found in Isaiah 53:10: "When thou shalt make his soul an offering for sin, he shall see his seed." In other words, when we make Christ's soul an offering for our sins—when we make the Atonement effective in our lives through faith, repentance, baptism, and enduring to the end in righteousness and charity—we become His seed, for then we are spiritually begotten of Him. King Benjamin beautifully explained the doctrine to his people who had covenanted to follow Christ: "And now, because of the covenant which ye have made ye shall be called the children of Christ, his sons, and his daughters; for behold, this day he hath spiritually begotten you; for ye say that your hearts are changed through faith on his name; therefore, ye are born of him and have become his sons and his daughters" (Mosiah 5:7).

Is it possible, then, for Christ to be both our brother and our father? Can He really be both the Father and the Son? Latter-day Saints understand that not only is it possible but it is essential for all who hope to gain exaltation. As the Son of God, He is our brother, and as we partake of His atoning sacrifice, He becomes the Father of our salvation.

QUESTIONS TO PONDER

1. How would an understanding of this prophecy have benefited people in the meridian of time?

2. Why was it necessary for Christ to be a "man of sorrows" and "acquainted with grief"? (53:3).

3. What other verbs could replace "pleased" in 53:10?

Chapter 51

"SING, O BARREN"

ISAIAH 54

In Isaiah 54 the prophet returns to a remarkable prophecy given earlier—a prophecy that the time will come when the ensign, or gospel, will be raised up among certain Gentiles who will then help gather scattered and lost Israel, restore them to the covenants, and be recognized as part of the covenant family (see 11:10–16; 49:18–23). In Isaiah 54 Israel is likened to a married but barren wife who will break forth into singing as she learns that though she has not labored in childbirth, a desolate one shall bring forth covenant children in abundance—so many that they will be compelled to enlarge their dwellings to accommodate them all (54:1–3). In comforting and assuring tones the Lord promises His children that this is all according to His divine plan. Though they have strayed from Him and were forsaken and refused for a time, when they return to honor their covenants with Him, the Lord, as their divine husband, intends to have mercy on them, gather them, restore them, protect them, and redeem them, just as surely as the mountains endure and as surely as He has kept His covenant to Noah never to destroy the earth by flood again (54:4–17).

LIKENING ISAIAH'S WORDS UNTO OURSELVES

Who is the desolate one who will, much to the surprise and delight of the barren married wife, bring forth so many children that the tents of the covenant people will be bursting at the seams? (54:1–3). As Latter-day Saints we can see ourselves as a fulfillment of this marvelous promise. We may be deemed desolate by those who do not understand that we are the prophesied Gentiles among whom the ensign has been raised and who have the mandate to assist in gathering and restoring scattered Israel, the barren married wife (11:10–16; see discussion of Isaiah 49). But as they are restored to the covenant, gathered Israel will delight to know that one thought to be desolate is in truth part of the covenant family, a vital part through whom the Lord has been fulfilling His promises. They will come to know that though "the mountains shall depart, and the hills be removed," the Lord's "kindness shall not depart from thee, neither shall the covenant of my peace be removed" (54:10). We can help the Lord accomplish this important work with hopefulness and happiness.

QUESTIONS TO PONDER

1. Do the Lord's promises in 54:4–10 concerning Zion as a whole apply on a personal level as well? How?

2. How has the promise of 54:17 been realized today?

Chapter 52

"COME YE, BUY, . . . WITHOUT MONEY"

ISAIAH 55

Fervent and tender invitations characterize Isaiah 55. All who thirst are invited to partake of the Lord's water, wine, and milk, which can be bought without money or price and will help them avoid laboring for that which is not bread and does not satisfy (55:1–2). We are invited to "hearken diligently" so that we can eat "that which is good" (55:2). We are then entreated to incline our ears and come unto the Lord with the promise that in doing so our souls shall live and we shall enter an everlasting covenant, receiving the sure mercies of David and the support of "a nation that thou knowest not" (55:5; compare 2 Samuel 7:15–17; Acts 13:26–41; Isaiah 49:18–23; 54:1–3). We are further invited to "seek" the Lord, "call upon" Him, and "return" unto Him with the assurance that He will have mercy and "abundantly pardon" (55:6–7). All this the Lord can do, for His thoughts and ways are higher than ours (55:8–9). He can perform His pleasure; control the elements; provide rain, seed, and bread as needed; and cause us to rejoice (55:10–13). He will do all this, for an "everlasting sign that shall not be cut off" (55:13).

LIKENING ISAIAH'S WORDS UNTO OURSELVES

The invitation to purchase and partake of the water, wine, and milk of the Lord without money or price reminds us that earlier the Lord declared that though we may sell "ourselves for nought," we can be "redeemed without money" (55:1; 52:3; compare 2 Nephi 2:4). The teachings invite us to ask, "How does one buy without money? What is the currency in which we make these trades? Is there really no cost to redemption?" Some answers to these questions can be found in the doctrine of salvation by grace (see, for example, Acts 15:11; Ephesians 2:8; 2 Nephi 10:24; 25:23).

Some understand this doctrine to mean that salvation is wholly a gift, a pure act of grace. Others add that we qualify to receive this grace, this gift of salvation, by doing all we can to love, serve, and obey God. After we have done all we can, God grants us salvation as an act of grace, not because we have earned—or even could earn—a gift as wonderful and priceless as salvation. Some also remind us that all are saved from physical death through the resurrection as an act of grace. All these ideas can help us conceptualize different ways we are saved by grace.

Isaiah's imagery of buying without price, or cost, suggests another way to understand salvation by grace. We recognize that each of us is deeply indebted to the Savior for His atoning sacrifice that makes salvation possible. Normally when we are indebted to another we must repay the debt. For example, if we owe another person a thousand dollars, we are expected to pay him or her a thousand dollars. Though we may wish it, we can never make such a cash payment to the Savior for the debt we incurred when He suffered for us in Gethsemane and died for us at Golgotha. He has, however, taught us how to show our love and gratitude to Him. He taught, "If ye love me, keep my commandments" (John 14:15; compare D&C 42:29). "A new commandment I give unto you, that ye love one another; as I have loved you, that ye also love one another" (John 13:34). "Inasmuch as ye have done it unto one of the least of these my brethren, ye have done it unto me" (Matthew 25:40). Thus, in a sense, Christ invites us to show our desire to pay our debt to Him through our love, service, and obedience.

Typically when we pay a debt to a mortal creditor, we are diminished and our creditor enriched by the act. Returning to our example to illustrate the point, when we pay the thousand dollars we owe to our creditor, we are a thousand dollars poorer and the creditor is a thousand dollars wealthier. Our bank account is diminished, and the creditor's is enlarged. But that is not so when we show our desire to pay our debt to Christ, for as we do what He asks of us, as we love, serve, and obey, we are not diminished by the acts. Indeed, we are enriched by the process, for the acts of loving, serving and obeying enlarge us—they make us better. We emerge from this repayment process with more spiritual capital than when we began. Thus, "paying" our debt to the Savior costs us nothing. It only enriches us. As an act of grace, He bids us to "pay" our debt to Him by enriching ourselves. Truly, when we love and serve others, striving to obey God's commandments, we are purchasing His living water without price and are redeemed without cost.

QUESTIONS TO PONDER

1. How can we help the Lord extend the invitations of this chapter to others? Who in your life needs to hear and understand the invitations?

2. How would you summarize the message of 55:8–9? How should that message influence your decisions?

Chapter 53

"A PLACE AND A NAME"

ISAIAH 56

Isaiah 56 begins with a promise of blessings to the righteous, even a promise that the Lord's salvation is near and His righteousness is soon to be revealed. In contrast, the chapter ends with a frightening warning of destruction to the wicked, especially to those shepherds commissioned to be watchmen but who, instead of caring for the flock, are preoccupied with their own way and gain. We can feel the Lord's anger with such selfish servants as He labels them "blind," "ignorant," and "dumb dogs" that cannot bark a warning in their slothful slumber, condemning them as "greedy dogs" and "shepherds that cannot understand" as they indulge themselves in their reveling (56:9–12).

Between the promise and the warning is a message to the sons of the stranger and the eunuch, promising remarkable blessings to them if they keep the Sabbath and choose the things that please God (56:3–8).

LIKENING ISAIAH'S WORDS UNTO OURSELVES

To Isaiah's contemporaries a stranger was one outside their people or nation—a foreigner, or Gentile. Because both the sons

158

of the stranger and the eunuch were not typically thought to be part of the covenant people, the promises given to them in Isaiah 56 are remarkable. To those willing to accept the gospel, the Lord promised to "give in mine house and within my walls a place and a name better than of sons and of daughters: I will give them an everlasting name" (56:5). The phrase "place and a name" is more accurately translated as "hand and a name." As the Lord brings them to his holy mountain, He assures that there He will "make them joyful in my house of prayer" and promises that they will be able to participate in temple ordinances, for "their burnt offerings and their sacrifices shall be accepted upon mine altar; for mine house shall be called an house of prayer for all people" (56:7).

The thought that Gentiles could participate in temple worship would have astonished Isaiah's contemporaries, for under the dictates of the Mosaic law they observed, they were not allowed to enter the inner parts of the sanctuary. Only priests could perform temple rites, and only the high priest entered the most holy part of the temple. But here Isaiah foretells of a day when all, even Gentiles and eunuchs, who serve and love the Lord could enter His house and be given a hand and a name that would make them equal to the sons and daughters born into the covenant people (56:3–7). The prophet describes a truly wonderful day and a truly significant doctrine, the doctrine that ultimately righteousness, not genealogy, determines election.

Latter-day Saints see the fulfillment of this prophecy in temple worship today. Just as Isaiah prophesied, all who are willing to "join themselves to the Lord, to serve him, and to love the name of the Lord, to be his servants, every one that keepeth the sabbath from polluting it, and taketh hold of [the Lord's] covenant" may qualify to enter the temple, even the most holy parts thereof, and participate in temple worship, there being endowed with a "name," even "an everlasting name, that shall not be cut off" (56:6–7; compare 2 Nephi 26:33).

QUESTIONS TO PONDER

1. How would you teach someone about the meaning of the phrase to take "hold of my covenant," as used in 56:6?

2. What responsibilities of a watchman do you have? How do you avoid the problems that plagued those described in 56:9–12?

Chapter 54

"HE SHALL ENTER INTO PEACE"

ISAIAꞨ 57

A contrast between the peace and confidence enjoyed by the righteous and the turmoil and trouble endured by the wicked characterizes Isaiah 57. The righteous do not fear death, and their sleep is peaceful (57:1–2). They shall "possess the land, and shall inherit" the Lord's "holy mountain" (57:13). The Lord will remove stumbling blocks out of their way and revive their hearts and spirits (57:13–15). They will be led, comforted, and healed by the Lord (57:18–19). They experience the peace that comes from knowing they are right with their God (57:19).

In contrast, the wicked, particularly those who are caught up in sorcery, idolatry, and immorality (57:3–9), can expect no such peace as they "debase [themselves] even unto hell" (57:9). They will find themselves weary and unable to grieve for or even recognize their hopeless state (57:10–12). Their cries will fall upon unhearing ears (57:13) as they incur the wrath of God and are smitten of Him (57:16–17). They are like a "troubled sea, when it cannot rest, whose waters cast up mire and dirt" (57:20). "There is no peace," the Lord declares, "to the wicked" (57:21).

LIKENING ISAIAH'S WORDS UNTO OURSELVES

In its fullest sense, the Hebrew term *shalom,* translated as "peace" in Isaiah 57 (vv. 2, 11, 19, 21), means much more than an absence of war. Depending on the context, *shalom* can also connote wholeness, completeness, health, safety, happiness, friendliness, prosperity, rest, blessedness, quietness, justice, confidence, and/or perfection. In the context of this chapter, it seems that all the various meanings apply. The hope and faith of the righteous can provide them *shalom*—make them complete, happy, peaceful, and confident in spirit, body, and mind, even in the face of life's trials, in a way that those who have estranged themselves from God can never understand or appreciate (for example, 57:10). Indeed, God lives in *shalom* and has held His "peace even of old" (57:11). His work and His glory are to "dwell in the high and holy place" in *shalom* with His righteous children (57:15). This peace, this *shalom,* stands in stark contrast to the Lord's statement in Isaiah 56:21 that there is no peace to the wicked. Each of us is free to choose either the peace that accompanies righteous living or the absence of *shalom* that attends the wicked.

QUESTIONS TO PONDER

1. How is the peace described in Isaiah 57 manifested in your life?

2. If God loves us, why will He not grant such peace to the wicked as well?

Chapter 55

"THEN SHALL THY LIGHT BREAK FORTH"

ISAIAH 58

I saiah 58 is a remarkable discussion of fasting and Sabbath Day observance. The Lord begins by describing the improper and hypocritical fasting of His people, identifying it as a sin among them (58:1–5). He next describes what constitutes a proper fast (58:6–7). In beautiful poetic language, He speaks of the blessings that come from righteous, sincere fasting (58:8–12).

Following His discussion of proper fasting, the Lord turns His attention to proper Sabbath observance. He explains principles of Sabbath observance that can make the day "a delight" (58:13). Again in stirring language He speaks of the blessings that come from faithful Sabbath observance (58:14).

LIKENING ISAIAH'S WORDS UNTO OURSELVES

Is it possible for fasting to take us farther from God rather than closer to Him? The Lord's instructions revealed through Isaiah in chapter 58 indicate yes! Fasting can be a wonderful means of gaining spiritual strength and direction, but it is also possible for us to fast ineffectively, even sinfully. There appears to be a difference between fasting and simply going hungry. Accordingly, we should be deeply interested in this difference between real, effective fasting and the mere hypocritical abstaining from food described in this passage.

As the Lord responds to those who were complaining that He had not noticed or rewarded their fasting, He explains why their efforts had been ineffective. Their fasting was self-centered. They used their day of fasting to do as they pleased, to draw attention to themselves, and to get others to labor for them (58:3). They got cranky when they were fasting, complaining and arguing with one another, even coming to blows (58:4). Some wanted everyone to marvel at their piety in fasting, letting the world know by raising their voices and covering themselves with sackcloth and ashes. Their thoughts, actions, and concerns all seemed to be turned inward. It makes us wonder if we know anyone today who has similar problems in fasting—anyone in our Church—anyone in our family—perhaps ourselves?

The Lord's instructions about what constitutes a proper fast are inspiring and can be life-changing if we follow them. He explains that our fasting needs to have a purpose. For example, we can fast to help ourselves and others find strength to overcome weaknesses, to loosen "the bands of wickedness," to undo "heavy burdens," to free the "oppressed," and to "break every yoke" (58:6). The temptations, trials, tragedies, sins, and sorrows of mortality can indeed bind, burden, oppress, and yoke us, but the Lord tells us that fasting can give us the strength, power, and perspective we need to persist in faith.

The Lord further instructs that rather than withdrawing and hiding as we fast, we should look for ways to help others, such as dealing our bread to the hungry and providing housing for the poor and clothing for the naked (58:7, 10). We do this today by being generous in our fast offerings, contributing what we can to the funds used to assist those who are in need. In an effective fast, our thoughts and actions are turned outwards rather than inwards.

Thus, in addition to abstaining from food for a period of time, a proper fast also includes fasting for a purpose and caring for others. Wonderful promises are given to us if we fast as the Lord instructs. Our "light," or truth, knowledge, and intelligence (D&C 93:24–37), will "break forth as the morning," surely arising each day and growing brighter as the day proceeds (58:8). Our health will improve, springing "forth speedily" (58:8). We will be protected as our righteousness goes before us and the "glory of the Lord" is our rereward, guiding, warning and defending us from behind (58:8). When we call unto our God, He will hear us, answering, "Here I am" (58:9). We will find light even in our darkest hours and living water and sustenance to satisfy our souls (58:10–11). We and our children will be able to raise up, build up, and restore the foundations and paths that will lead us to dwell with our God (58:12). Surely, fasting is a simple act of worship that yields profound returns.

QUESTIONS TO PONDER

1. Can you identify times in your life when you have experienced the blessings of proper fasting described in 58:8–12? When and how?

2. How would you summarize the principles of proper Sabbath observance described in 58:13?

Chapter 56

"THEY HATCH
COCKATRICE EGGS"

ISAIAH 59

Isaiah 59 returns to the message of judgment and warning that heavily flavored the first thirty-five chapters of Isaiah. The prophet bemoans the separation that the people's sins have created between them and God (59:1–2; compare 50:1). He describes the sins that have led to their estrangement (59:3–8) and the sorrowful resignation the people will feel as they come to recognize all that they have lost as a consequence of their iniquities (59:9–15). Isaiah then reveals how the Lord will respond to the choices of His people (59:16–21). Those who rebelliously misuse their agency will reap His fury and vengeance (59:15–19), whereas those who turn from transgression will find His salvation and redemption (16–17; 20–21). Thus the Lord will either be the Avenger or the Redeemer. The role He plays depends upon us.

LIKENING ISAIAH'S WORDS UNTO OURSELVES

The prophet Alma warned Zeezrom and the apostate people of Ammonihah, "Our *words* will condemn us, yea, all our *works* will condemn us; we shall not be found spotless; and our *thoughts* will also condemn us; and in this awful state we shall not dare to look up to our God" (Alma 12:14; emphasis added; compare Mosiah 4:30). Alma's warning that we will be judged by our words, works, and thoughts echoes the warning given centuries earlier by Isaiah to the wicked among his people. Among Isaiah's contemporaries were those whose words condemned them, for their lips had "spoken lies" and their tongues had "muttered perverseness" (59:3, 13). Their works also condemned them, for their "hands" were "defiled with blood" and their "fingers with iniquity" (59:3, 6). Likewise their thoughts condemned them, for they conceived "mischief" and were "thoughts of iniquity" (59:4, 7). Isaiah likened their brooding over evil thoughts to hatching the eggs of a cockatrice (a venomous snake) and weaving spider webs. Eventually such thoughts would produce "works of iniquity" that would do them harm, even vipers to bite them and webs to ensnare them (59:5–6), leaving them to "roar all like bears, and mourn sore like doves" in their anguish (59:11).

We wonder why anyone would be foolish enough to hatch the eggs of a deadly cockatrice. Then again, why would anyone incubate venomous thoughts that poison the soul and lead to spiritually destructive words and acts? Isaiah tells us that evil and poisonous thoughts need to be removed, destroyed, ignored, or abandoned, just as surely as the eggs of a creature that could kill us should be destroyed or safely isolated away from us. His warning makes excellent sense, for thoughts precede actions and words. As we control our thoughts, we control our words and deeds, thereby better preparing ourselves to meet our God as our Redeemer rather than as the Avenger.

QUESTIONS TO PONDER

1. How does the judgment dialogue of 59:12 compare with 2 Nephi 9:14? What does it tell us about our role in the Last Judgment?

2. How do you deal with your own cockatrice eggs?

Chapter 57

"THE SONS OF STRANGERS
SHALL BUILD UP THY WALLS"

ISAIAH 60

A prophecy of restoration and redemption bursts forth in chapter 60. Isaiah declares that after a period of apostasy and "gross darkness" the "Lord shall arise upon thee, and his glory shall be seen" (60:1–2). Gentiles will come to the light and sons and daughters will be gathered from afar (60:3–9). Together they will rebuild and restore (60:10–17). A theocracy of peace will follow. Violence will disappear. The Lord will be our light, and all shall be righteous (60:18–22).

LIKENING ISAIAH'S WORDS UNTO OURSELVES

As Isaiah describes this magnificent period of restoration and gathering, he again emphasizes the vital and central role that faithful latter-day Gentiles will play in the work (see discussion of Isaiah 49). As they are drawn to the light of the Lord they will be recognized as sons and daughters (60:3–4; compare 49:18–23; 54:1–3). Their sacrifices will be accepted upon the altar of the Lord's house (60:7; compare 56:3–7). They will build the walls and gates of Zion, nursing scattered Israel back into

169

the knowledge that the Lord, the mighty one of Jacob, is their Redeemer and Savior (60:10–16).

   As Gentiles who have the privilege of being stewards of the gospel in this dispensation, Latter-day Saints find in this prophecy direction, hope, promise, and a mandate to be its fulfillment.

QUESTIONS TO PONDER

1. What is the light that draws you to Christ? (60:3).

2. Who are the "sons of strangers" described in 60:10? What are the walls they are to build?

Chapter 58

"TO GIVE UNTO THEM BEAUTY FOR ASHES"

ISAIAH 61

A prophecy of a ministering, liberating, loving, and nurturing Messiah opens Isaiah (vv. 1–3), followed by an inspiring description of the blessings to be received and the labors to be performed by those comforted and redeemed by Him (61:4–6). Again Isaiah emphasizes the vital role Gentiles will play in the Messiah's plans, as strangers build and make productive a lost and scattered people, feeding their flocks, plowing their fields, and caring for their vineyards (61:5). They too will receive a divine inheritance and enjoy the blessings of the Lord's everlasting covenant, as the Lord causes righteousness and praise to spring forth before all the nations (61:1–11; the Hebrew word *goyim,* translated as "nations" in verse 11 is the same word translated as "Gentiles" elsewhere in Isaiah).

LIKENING ISAIAH'S WORDS UNTO OURSELVES

Luke tells us that early in Jesus' public ministry He returned to His hometown of Nazareth and spoke in the synagogue there. As He began His message to the villagers among whom He had grown up, He quoted a portion of Isaiah 61:1–2 (Luke 4:16–19).

This passage was likely well known and much beloved by Christ's contemporaries in the synagogue that day. Living at a subsistence level and having endured centuries of political oppression and captivity, the peasants of Nazareth would have longed for the advent of the promised anointed one, the Messiah who would bind up their broken hearts, open the prisons, and set them free (61:1–2). Sadly, however, even though Jesus told them that He was the Christ, their Messiah, their faith was insufficient to recognize the truth. They did not believe it possible. Rather than rejoicing in His declaration to them, the unbelieving Nazarenes sought to kill Him, deeming Him guilty of blasphemy (Luke 4:20–30). Thus a marvelous opportunity passed them by. Because those Nazarenes would not give their hearts a chance to believe, they forfeited the blessings promised in this beautiful prophecy.

In our day we are anxiously anticipating the return of the promised Messiah. Like the Jews of Nazareth that day centuries ago, we also long for His coming, but if our faith is sufficient we need not wait for His return to enjoy the wonderful blessings promised in this passage. Even now, if we are willing to allow our hearts a chance to believe, we can study the good tidings He taught, as recorded in the scriptures. Even now, we can find peace and perspective in Him when our hearts are broken, when we mourn and are in need of comfort. Even now, though the trials and challenges of mortality or our own foolish mistakes can turn our lives to ashes, He can give us "beauty for ashes" and "the oil of joy for mourning" (61:3). Even now, if we will love, trust, and follow Him, He will liberate us from sin and spiritual death.

QUESTIONS TO PONDER

1. How does Christ give us beauty for ashes? (61:3).

2. How can we be clothed as described in 61:10?

Chapter 59

"FOR JERUSALEM'S SAKE I WILL NOT REST"

ISAIAH 62

With eloquent imagery Isaiah 62 presents a prophetic picture of the restored and redeemed "daughter of Zion." The Lord assures Zion that He will not rest until His work of righteousness and salvation has gone forth and is recognized—until He and His people are joyfully united under the covenant (62:1–5). He further pledges that the watchmen He has commissioned to assist in the work will likewise not rest until He establishes and makes Jerusalem a praise in the earth (62:6–7). Then will His people be able to peacefully enjoy the fruits of their labors. The chapter closes with an imperative to His servants helping in the redemptive work to prepare for the coming salvation by casting up the highway, removing the stones thereof, and lifting up the standard, or ensign, for the people (62:10–12).

LIKENING ISAIAH'S WORDS UNTO OURSELVES

Isaiah and his contemporaries lived in a treacherous and insecure world. At any time a marauding nation could sweep through one's city or village, destroy all that one had built, kill loved ones, and carry off neighbors into slavery, simply because they had the might to do so. Spiritual upheaval was likewise a constant threat. Rulers and peasants alike often forsook Jehovah to worship other gods and idols. Prophets were frequently rejected. Materialism rather than righteousness often dictated decisions. Charity too often failed.

Many in our day face similar challenges. For some, survival is tenuous because they live in constant fear of attack, abuse, or displacement. Many in our modern world face spiritual challenges as they struggle to believe in God or to find reason for moral behavior. Today, too, charity often wanes as the love of men waxes cold in their pursuit of wealth, fame, power, and prestige.

When faced with such trial and turmoil we may wonder if God knows or cares about our struggles. We can find comfort in Isaiah's assurance that God does indeed know and care. We can have faith that "his reward is with him, and his work before him" (62:11). We can find peace in the promise that God and His watchmen are laboring on our behalf and will not rest until our salvation comes (62:6, 11–12).

QUESTIONS TO PONDER

1. Why does the Lord use watchmen? (62:6). Who is fulfilling this role in our day?

2. How are the servants' duties described in 62:10 accomplished in our era?

Chapter 60

"IN ALL THEIR AFFLICTION HE WAS AFFLICTED"

ISAIAR 63

Isaiah 63 opens with a fascinating dialogue between the returning millennial Messiah and some apparently apprehensive and bewildered mortals who encounter Him. As He comes in glory and strength from the direction of Edom, the confused people ask His identity and why His apparel is stained red (63:1–2). In response, the Lord identifies Himself as the one "mighty to save" (63:1). Then with vivid imagery the Messiah declares His garments are stained with blood from treading the "winepress alone," trampling the wicked in His fury in the "day of vengeance" and ushering in the "year of my redeemed" (63:3–4).

In the middle of chapter 63, the prophecy dramatically turns from a warning of vengeance and destruction for the wicked to a message of hope and loving kindness for the repentant and the redeemed. The prophet speaks of the Lord's mercy and suffering on behalf of His covenant people (63:7–9), notes their rebellion and chastisement (63:10), and foretells their repentance and return to faith as they remember how the Lord led and delivered them in the days of Moses (63:11–14).

A passage known as Isaiah's Intercessory Prayer closes this chapter and opens the next (63:15–64:12). This beautiful and instructive prayer will be discussed with Isaiah 64.

LIKENING ISAIAH'S WORDS UNTO OURSELVES

The image of our Savior in garments stained red with blood can be both frightening and humbling. Evil men are terrified as they realize that their own wicked blood, trampled from them in the Lord's fury and vengeance, will be shed upon His raiment. In stark contrast, the faithful and penitent are humbled as the image directs their thoughts to Gethsemane and Calvary, where our Savior suffered for all "that they might not suffer if they would repent," which suffering caused Him to "tremble because of pain, and to bleed at every pore" (D&C 19:16, 19). There too He trod "the winepress alone," staining His garments red with His blood, shed in our behalf (63:3). There "in all [our] affliction he was afflicted" (63:9).

Thus, how we feel as we contemplate the vision of Christ in red garments tells us much about our relationship with Him. Do we live in fear that His raiment will be turned crimson by our own rebellious blood shed in His wrath? Or are we filled with gratitude and love in the realization that His robes were once turned red by His blood spilt to redeem us? How wonderful it is to know that we can decide whether Christ's red garments are a sign of His love or a symbol of His wrath.

QUESTIONS TO PONDER

1. What do you think the Lord means by the phrase "I have trodden the winepress alone"? (63:3). Why?

2. How do Hebrews 2:16–18 and Alma 7:11–12 inform your understanding of Isaiah 63:9?

Chapter 61

"WE ARE THE CLAY, AND THOU OUR POTTER"

ISAIAH 64

As the Savior met with His disciples in the upper room shortly before descending to the agony of Gethsemane, He pleaded with the Father in their behalf. His petition is often referred to as Christ's Intercessory Prayer (John 17). In similar fashion, as Isaiah approaches the close of his book of prophecy, he offers a poignant plea to the Father that is known as Isaiah's Intercessory Prayer (63:15–64:12). Therein the prophet entreats God for intervention and mercy, acknowledges Him as our Father, recognizes His power and glory, confesses Israel's sins, and pleads for forgiveness and restoration (63:15–19).

LIKENING ISAIAH'S WORDS UNTO OURSELVES

As Isaiah appeals to God he humbly testifies, "O Lord, thou art our father; we are the clay, and thou our potter" (64:8). The testimony speaks volumes about the depth of Isaiah's commitment to God and the way he lived his life. When he declared, "Here am I; send me" (6:8–13) in answer to the Lord's call for one to be a prophet to a stubborn and rebellious people, Isaiah placed his agency in God's hands. He demonstrated his trust that God would take him and shape him and make him into a vessel worthy to assist in His redeeming work. Isaiah recognized that God is the supreme craftsman, who will, if we are willing to be clay in His hands, mold us into something far greater than we could ever make of ourselves. What a marvelous blessing it is to know that the hand that fashioned the universe is also willing to shape and form and make perfect the small bit of clay we have to offer Him.

QUESTIONS TO PONDER

1. How can we allow God to mold us? (64:8).

2. What will be the product of the molding?

3. How are we fulfilling our role in the process?

Chapter 62

"THESE ARE SMOKE
IN MY NOSE"

ISAIAH 65

At the end of Isaiah 65 we are given an intriguing description of millennial life. Joy will abound in the holy city; people will not die before their time; homes will be built; land will be cultivated and the produce thereof enjoyed by those who tend it (65:17–23). Peace will prevail, and the Lord will hear and answer prayers even as they are offered (65:23–25).

Yet this description of millennial bliss stands in stark contrast to the withering rebuke the Lord gives at the beginning of the chapter. He chastises the covenant people for their hypocrisy, noting that He is more readily sought and found by a nation that was not called by His name, perhaps again foreshadowing the conversion of faithful Gentiles in the latter-days (65:1–7).

The Lord then reassures the covenant people that in spite of their rebellion, He will yet raise up a righteous and elect remnant from among them (65:8–10). He warns that those who persist in iniquity, those who choose not to be part of the righteous remnant, will be destroyed and enjoy none of the blessings reserved for His servants (65:11–16), even the joy of the millennial life He so beautifully describes (65:17–23).

LIKENING ISAIAH'S WORDS UNTO OURSELVES

Certain hazards or pitfalls can plague a covenant people. The Lord identifies one that is particularly disturbing to Him as He chastises those of His people who, consumed with pride, dictate to others, "Stand by thyself, come not near to me; for I am holier than thou" (65:5). If they are not careful, those who identify themselves as part of the chosen people can easily become self-righteous, thinking they are superior to others and feeling justified in withdrawing from or ostracizing those they view as less worthy than themselves. Such an attitude is anathema to our God, who loves all of His children and whose whole work and glory are to bring them to immortality and eternal life.

The Lord describes those plagued with the "holier than thou" attitude as "smoke in my nose" (65:5). Those who have stood by a fire when a shifting wind blew smoke in their face will find this a vivid description of the Lord's disgust. As the smoke swirls about our faces, our eyes burn, we gag and are compelled to flee in search of fresher air. What a tragedy it would be if our God, looking upon us, was moved to turn away in distaste and disgust—as if we were smoke in His nose—because we mistakenly assumed that being part of a covenant people made us too good to care for or help others. A covenant people must always remember the principle of servant leadership: "Whosoever will be chief among you, let him be your servant" (Matthew 20:27). We must ever recall that "for of him unto whom much is given much is required" (D&C 82:3). We must demonstrate our understanding that being part of a chosen people should move us to engage more fully rather than disengage from helping God in His work to redeem others. Being part of a chosen people does not necessarily make one superior to others, but it does make one more responsible and accountable.

QUESTIONS TO PONDER

1. What attitudes and actions distinguish a servant from someone who is not a servant, according to 65:13–16?

2. How does millennial life compare to our life now? (65:19–24).

Chapter 63

"ALL FLESH SHALL COME TO WORSHIP BEFORE ME"

ISAIAH 66

As the book of Isaiah closes, the Lord summarizes His plans for His people. He will watch over those who are poor and of a contrite spirit and condemns the hypocrites, who have chosen their own ways and who delight in their abominations (66:1–6). The Lord describes the joy, comfort, and peace that will prevail among the righteous when He brings forth Zion, as well as the slaughter that will befall the wicked when He comes to plead with all flesh by fire and sword (66:5–17). He promises that He will gather out the faithful from among all nations and bring them to His holy mountain to worship (66:18–24).

LIKENING ISAIAH'S WORDS UNTO OURSELVES

Book of Mormon prophets often closed their records with urgent counsel to latter-day Gentiles, who, they understood, would play a vital role in the ultimate restoration and redemption of their people. As Nephi neared the end of his writings, he spoke of the latter days when righteous Gentiles would have the gospel with the responsibility to gather scattered Israel and others to the covenant (2 Nephi 30). In his closing chapter he pleaded with these Gentiles to be "reconciled unto Christ" (2 Nephi 33:9). Likewise, as Mormon engraved his final message upon the plates, he admonished his people to "lay hold upon the gospel of Christ" that will be set before them in the record brought to them by the Gentiles (Mormon 7:8). Moroni, too, as he abridged the Jaredite record, spoke of the critical role of latter-day Gentiles in God's plans and admonished them to faithfully carry out their God-given mandate (Ether 4:13; 12:22–28, 38–41).

That same urgency, hope, and concern for latter-day Gentiles can be found in the final passage of Isaiah. Here the Lord speaks of missionaries sent out to the nations to "declare my glory among the Gentiles" (66:19). He explains that those of the Gentiles who accept the gospel will be recognized as "brethren" and will be privileged to partake of temple blessings, for they will be "clean vessels" whom the Lord will take for "priests and for Levites" (66:20–21). Then, the Lord assures, "shall all flesh come to worship before me" (66:23).

Faithful Latter-day Saints are a fulfillment of this prophecy. We become part of the covenant family as we accept the gospel, with the privilege of partaking of the fulness of its blessings and the mandate to help our God gather, restore, and redeem His children. We are the hope of great prophets who saw and rejoiced in our day.

QUESTIONS TO PONDER

1. What makes the difference between the individual described in 66:2 and the one described in 66:3?

2. If you have felt it in your own life, how would you define and describe the river-like peace discussed in 66:12?

3. What is your place and role in the final scene described by the prophet in Isaiah 66?

CONCLUSION

In studying Isaiah you likely have noticed many recurring themes in the prophet's words. Some have likened this book of scripture to a fugue, a musical composition in which a theme or melody is rendered in many different voices or variations, for in it we find recurring themes that give us hope, inspiration, and guidance. Isaiah confirms that God lives and is involved in our lives, that He has the power, knowledge, presence, and love to save us. He testifies that God allows us agency—the right to choose and learn from the consequences of our choices. He witnesses that God is just—chastising us for disobedience. He also testifies that God is merciful—forgiving us when we repent. The prophet Isaiah promises peace, joy, protection, and blessings as we humbly trust God and strive to do His will. He assures us that God has a plan to gather, restore and redeem His people. He promises that the millennial Messiah will indeed return to establish a theocracy of peace.

Isaiah composed some of the most beautiful and touching language in all scripture to describe the second coming of Christ and His reign as the millennial Messiah. In concluding our study of Isaiah, we have taken the liberty of compiling some of the millennial language scattered throughout Isaiah's writings into a single continuous narrative. We invite you to read it slowly and carefully, pondering the message of each phrase:

> The Redeemer shall come to Zion, and unto them that turn from transgression (59:20); he shall judge among the nations, and shall rebuke many people (2:4); of the increase of his government and peace there shall be no end, upon the throne of David, and upon his kingdom, to order it, and to establish it with judgment and with justice from henceforth even for ever (9:7); they shall beat their swords into plowshares, and their spears into pruninghooks: nation shall not lift up sword against nation, neither shall they learn war any more (2:4); violence shall no more be heard in thy land, wasting nor destruction within thy borders; but thou shalt call thy walls Salvation, and thy gates Praise. The sun shall be no more thy light by day; neither for brightness shall the moon give light unto thee: but the Lord shall be unto thee an everlasting light, and thy God thy glory (60: 18–19); the wolf also shall dwell with the lamb, and the leopard shall lie down with the kid . . . they shall not hurt nor destroy in all my holy mountain: for the earth shall be full of the knowledge of the Lord, as the waters cover the sea (11:6, 9); the ransomed of the Lord shall return, and come to Zion with songs and everlasting joy upon their heads: they shall obtain joy and gladness, and sorrow and sighing shall flee away (35:10); in that day shall the branch of the Lord be beautiful and glorious, and the fruit of the earth shall be excellent and comely for them that are escaped of Israel. And it shall come to pass, that he that is left in Zion, and he that remaineth in Jerusalem, shall be called holy, even every one

that is written among the living (4:2–3); thine eyes shall see the king in his beauty: they shall behold the land that is very far off (33:17); he will swallow up death in victory; and the Lord God will wipe away tears from off all faces (25:8); to give unto them beauty for ashes, the oil of joy for mourning, the garment of praise for spirit of heaviness (61:3); then the eyes of the blind shall be opened, and the ears of the deaf shall be unstopped (35:5); he shall feed his flock like a shepherd: he shall gather the lambs with his arm, and carry them in his bosom (40:11); and it shall be said in that day, Lo, this is our God; we have waited for him, and he will save us: this is the Lord; we have waited for him (25:9).

We hope this collection of millennial promises gives you inspiration and perspective as you "wait upon the Lord" (40:31). We further hope the insights we have offered help you find application for the prophet Isaiah's teachings in your life and give you tools to help you teach and share this remarkable book of scripture with your family, friends, loved ones, and others. We especially hope this volume has strengthened both your ability and desire to follow the Savior's admonition to search the words of Isaiah (3 Nephi 23:1).

SOURCES CITED

Brown, Francis, S. R. Driver, and Charles A. Briggs. *The New Brown-Driver-Briggs-Gesenius Hebrew and English Lexicon with an Appendix Containing the Biblical Aramaic.* Peabody, Mass.: Hendrickson, 1979.

Hymns of The Church of Jesus Christ of Latter-day Saints. Salt Lake City: The Church of Jesus Christ of Latter-day Saints, 1985.

Josephus, Flavius. *The Antiquities of the Jews.* In *Josephus: Complete Works.* Translated by William Whiston. Grand Rapids, Mich.: Kregel Publications, 1960.

Journal of Discourses. 26 vols. London: Latter-day Saints Book Depot, 1854–86.

Kimball, Spencer W. *Faith Precedes the Miracle.* Salt Lake City: Deseret Book, 1972.

INDEX